The Ships of
PEMBROKE DOCKYARD

The Ships of

PEMBROKE DOCKYARD

PHIL CARRADICE

AMBERLEY

First published 2013

Amberley Publishing
The Hill, Stroud
Gloucestershire, GL5 4EP

www.amberley-books.com

British Library Cataloguing in Publication Data.
A catalogue record for this book is available from the British Library.

ISBN 978 1 4456 1290 4
E-book ISBN 978 1 4456 1310 9

Typeset in 10pt on 12pt Sabon.
Typesetting and Origination by Amberley Publishing.
Printed in the UK.

Contents

Acknowledgements

Thanks, first and foremost, to the shipwrights, smithies and workers of Pembroke Dockyard who built the ships – without them there would be no story. With limited resources and few facilities, they performed miracles, producing some of the finest ships in the nineteenth and early twentieth century Royal Navy. Thanks to Roger MacCallum for his knowledge of Pembroke Dock history and his expertise with technology that, as usual, left me dumbfounded. Thanks to Trudy, my wife – as ever, supportive and encouraging.

ABOUT THE AUTHOR

Phil Carradice is one of Wales' best known authors. Poet, novelist and historian, he has published over forty books. He recently produced, for Amberley, *First World War in the Air* and *A Pembrokeshire Childhood in the 1950s*. A regular broadcaster on BBC radio and television, he also writes a weekly blog for BBC Wales History.

1

A Different Sort of History

There has been so much written – books and articles, fact and fiction – about the dockyard at Pembroke Dock that readers and potential book-buyers might be excused for thinking 'Oh no, not another one.' Even though the year 2014 marks the bicentenary of the dockyard and town, any new publication about such a well-covered subject needs to be different, very different indeed.

And so this book is exactly that – it is different. It concentrates not on the buildings and streets of the town, not even on the growth and decline of the yards, but on the ships that were created during the one hundred and twelve years that the dockyard was running. It covers their creation, their careers and, in many cases, their deaths as well.

During the century of its existence nearly three hundred ships were built at Pembroke Dock, the only Royal Naval dockyard ever to exist in Wales. It is hard to estimate the exact roll call of Pembroke Dock ships as new vessels come to light with relentless regularity. Quite apart from a whole bevy of lighters and tank vessels that slipped, almost unnoticed into the waters of the Haven, so many orders were placed and then cancelled by the Admiralty that the exact number fluctuates slightly with each list you survey.

More importantly, for this book at least, not all of those vessels had interesting or adventurous lives. As you might expect, some served briefly and uneventfully, vanishing into obscurity, causing the historian or interested reader to wonder if they ever actually existed.

Others, however, were destined to cover themselves in glory, in fame and sometimes, it must be admitted, utter disaster. These are the ships that form the nucleus, the essential focus, of this book.

Inevitably, there will have to be some mention of the dockyard at Pembroke Dock. Without some awareness of its development and decline, the ships and their stories would be left in limbo. Like any good history we have to know from whence we came if we are to see where we go in the future. It is the same with the ships discussed here and so the life of the yards, from creation to closure, is an important part of the story.

Above: Pembroke Dockyard, *c.* 1900, huge building sheds lining the water's edge – a classic view of the power, grace and grandeur that was once the Royal Naval Dockyard.

Left: A County Class cruiser, probably the *Essex*, sits alongside the fitting out berth at Hobbs Point at the beginning of the twentieth century. Note the huge sheer legs towering over the ship, the first vessel to be totally fitted out at Pembroke Dock.

In the main, however, the emphasis is on the ships and their careers, usually far away from the dockyard that built them as they flew the flag in distant and far-flung parts of the British Empire.

Most Pembroke Dock ships slid easily down the slipways and, after their launch – and usually before fitting out – were towed out of Milford Haven, never to return. Yet they were Pembroke Dock ships and would remain so until the day they were finally broken up or vanished forever beneath the waves they had been created to traverse.

Only two major conflicts took place during the short life of Pembroke Dockyard – the Crimean War of 1854–56 and the Great War of 1914–18. However, there were many 'little wars' during that period, an almost constant series of skirmishes as the Empire slowly extended its reach, and Pembroke Dock ships were involved in nearly all of these colonial conflicts, performing with greater or lesser degrees of success.

In many cases it is these small engagements that provide the most fascinating stories. Apart from its lumbering men of war and, later, the giant pre-dreadnought battleships that the yards produced, the stream of small frigates, sloops and gunboats launched from Pembroke Dockyard were designed to show the force of British arms across the world. The numerous actions in which they were involved helped give the Royal Navy a standing that has hardly been equalled, either before or since.

While the main thrust of this book is in the stories – the stories of the ships and the men who sailed them – it is perhaps appropriate at this point to give a warning. Do not look here for technical details of length, breadth, displacement, tonnage and so on. They may well be mentioned, if such detail is relevant, but it is the stories of the ships, their histories, that take centre stage.

The human element remains equally as fascinating. Bravery, courage, foolishness and cowardice, they all add another dimension to the stories and tales. The life of a sailor in the nineteenth century was unbelievably dangerous and as Dr Johnson, irascible and bad tempered as ever, once declared:

No man will be a sailor who has contrivance enough to get himself into a jail, for being in a ship is like being in a jail, with the chance of being drowned.[1]

He undoubtedly had a point. Taking just one year as an example, Board of Trade figures for 1861 show that the death toll of sailors was 4,000 in that twelve month period – one in fifty-six of all those who went to sea. In that same year the equivalent death rate for miners, traditionally one of the most dangerous of all jobs, was a mere one in three hundred and fifty. [2]

In the days of sail, ships were equipped with huge amounts of canvas. To operate them large numbers of men were needed. The frigate *Arethusa* of 1849, for example, may have been only 180 foot in length but she still required a crew of 500 in order to sail her effectively. And those 500 men had to live, sleep and work in the wettest, dirtiest and most cramped conditions you can ever imagine. Small wonder that diseases such as TB and typhus (carried by the human body louse and endemic where there were no proper washing facilities or decent clothing) were rife on board such ships.

Food was awful, the meat usually rotten after a week at sea, so that the sailors invariably had to resort to hard tack and biscuit. Even when the ship was in port and fresh fruit and meat were readily available there were still 'meatless days' in the weekly ration, a particularly mindless infliction that was to hit sailors hard for a large part of the nineteenth century. Water was often contaminated – small wonder that the daily issue of rum and beer was looked forward to with relish.

The fact that sailors were not provided with cutlery until the end of the nineteenth century gives a fair indication of society's feelings towards the men who crewed the

Merchant and Royal Navy fleets. There was no such thing as leave, by right rather than as a privilege, until 1890. Such a lack of consideration was a clear 'hangover' from the days of the Press Gang when to grant leave to men who had been taken on board ship by force rather than choice would be to invite wholesale desertion.

As if to reinforce the harsh nature of a sailor's life, corporal punishment, in the form of public beatings on the deck of the ship, remained the main form of corrective treatment long after Victoria came to the throne.

In the first two or three decades of the nineteenth century the Press Gang remained a potent and much-feared force. Whenever there was a ship to be crewed parties of sailors, usually under the command of some hapless midshipman, roamed all coastal towns looking for 'recruits' into the Royal Navy. Sailors homeward bound after a voyage of many months or even years certainly had good reason to fear the 'pressing cutters' that lurked around the mouth of rivers and estuaries like the Thames.

Given the conditions that sailors had to endure it is a wonder that the Royal Navy ever found anyone to crew its ships – one of the reasons why the Press Gang was forced to operate, legally and with official sanction, for many years. Yet serve they did and the men who sailed the Pembroke Dock ships into fire fights and typhoons are as worthy of recognition as the ships themselves.

Not all Pembroke Dock ships were uniformly successful. The yards were founded in a period of revolutionary change in ship design and tactics. When work began in 1814, ships simply pulled in as close as they could manage to the enemy fleet and blazed away with broadside after broadside. Of course there were tactics, Nelson's cutting the line of the French/Spanish fleet at Trafalgar being clear proof of that. But even so, in the main naval tactics consisted, as they had since the days of Francis Drake, Lord Howard and Martin Frobisher, of pummeling the enemy before he could do it to you.

When the dockyard closed in 1926 ships were firing projectiles from a distance of many miles, even sometimes from over the horizon. Submarines ranged beneath the waves, eager to pounce on any unsuspecting victim. Already, aircraft carriers were beginning to alter naval combat forever.

In what was probably the most revolutionary development of all, during the short life span of Pembroke Dockyard iron and steel had replaced wood as the main building material. Ships had been built out of wood for hundreds, even thousands of years, but by the middle decades of the nineteenth century the day of the timber built warship was over. And dockyards like Pembroke Dock, established to build those massive wooden warships, had to adapt quickly – or die!

Pembroke Dock had to cope with all of this. The wonder is not that the yards produced the occasional failure, rather that they managed to build anything of substance and value at all.

The story of the Pembroke Dock ships is fascinating and informative. In many respects, their stories echo those of so many other Victorian and Edwardian vessels – they might have been built in west Wales but they could have been built anywhere. They are, perhaps, the history of the Royal Navy, post-Trafalgar up to the end of the Great War, in microcosm. They encapsulate so much of the history of Britain in the nineteenth century.

The gates of the Dockyard, shut for once, on the occasion of the Investiture of the Prince of Wales in 1911.

Pembroke Dockyard in the 1850s, already established as one of the great British shipbuilding yards.

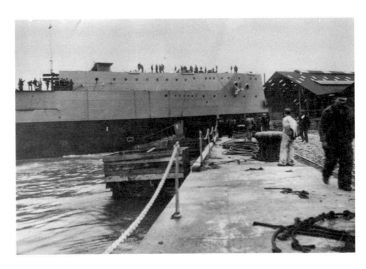

Pembroke Dockyard as it will always be remembered – the launch of the cruiser *Defence*.

2

Founding the Yards

The importance of Milford Haven, the sunken valley that connects to the River Cleddau just off the modern town of Pembroke Dock, has long been recognised. Richard Strongbow, son of the Earl of Pembroke, used the Haven as his base during the conquest of Ireland in the twelfth century while in 1172 Henry II supposedly gathered a fleet of 400 ships in the Haven prior to his campaign against the Irish. In 1405 and 1485 respectively, Owain Glyndwr and Henry Tudor both landed on beaches along the waterway, with the support of French mercenary soldiers.

Clearly then, the Haven was always a potential weak spot, the ideal place for any invasion of Britain but as late as the middle years of the eighteenth century little or nothing had been done about defending this soft underbelly.

In 1756, with Britain at war with France, a report by Colonel Bastide of the Royal Engineers suggested the building of six large defensive forts along the waterway but his recommendations were rejected as too expensive. An alternative plan of just three forts was put into operation but, in the event, only one was ever begun, at Paterchurch Point within a stone's throw of the future dockyard at Pembroke Dock. By 1759 the danger of a French invasion had passed and work on the fort was unceremoniously stopped.

Enter the town of Milford! It was developed as a business enterprise by Sir William Hamilton, a long term friend of Horatio Nelson and the cuckolded husband of the infamous Emma. The three of them actually lived together in a strange *menage a trois* for several years, a scandal that intrigued the British public but did little to harm Nelson's reputation.

Under the patronage of Hamilton and with the guidance of his nephew Charles Francis Greville, the new town began to grow and develop in the wake of the Milford Haven Harbour Act which was passed in 1790.

When, in 1796, the Navy Board which, along with the separate Admiralty Board, actually ran and directed the navy at this time, contracted with Messrs Harry and Joseph Jacob to build three new ships of war, the shipbuilders-come-businessmen turned to Milford as the base for their new enterprise.

Land was cleared, a labour force recruited and work duly began on the ships but, unfortunately, the Jacobs brothers' business soon failed and the owners were declared

Above: A rather fanciful artistic impression of Milford Haven, the waterway full of shipping and the town of Milford beginning to take shape in the distance.

Right: The man who, indirectly, was responsible for the founding of the yards at Pembroke Dock – Charles Francis Greville from a painting by George Romney

bankrupt. With ships on the stocks and, with the Revolutionary Wars with France raging hotter and harder than ever, the Navy Board simply took over the business and completed the vessels themselves.

The first three ships launched from this private yard were the 18-gun sloop *Nautilus* – wrecked in the Mediterranean in 1807 – the frigate *Lavinia* and the line of battle ship *Milford* which slipped into the waters of the Haven in 1809.

Importantly, the Admiralty did not own the land at Milford – they simply rented it from Charles Greville, who had succeeded to the estates on the death of Sir William Hamilton, on a year to year basis. Therefore, the shipbuilding enterprise was never a Royal Dockyard. However, by 1809 the yards were well established, there were regular and effective supply routes for the delivery of building materials such as timber and rope and, most important of all, there was now a trained and capable workforce on hand. And so the Navy Board decided to purchase the land from Greville and create a proper Royal Dockyard.

A price of £4,455 was agreed for the land but it took time for the technicalities and various approvals to work their way through the mire of officialdom. It was 11 October 1809 before an Order in Council granted permission for the purchase. And then disaster struck.

On 23 April 1809 Charles Greville had died and his brother, Robert Fulke Greville, his only heir, succeeded to the estates. When he had had time to survey his empire and consider his position, the new owner, perhaps greedy, perhaps realistic, decided that the previously agreed price was far too low and refused to accept the Navy Board's now fully approved offer. It was a collision of two heavyweights as Greville

Shipbuilding as it would have been at the embryonic Milford and, later, Pembroke Dockyards. The ship takes shape inside a wooden cradle or frame on the foreshore.

An early view of Milford Docks – the shipbuilding would probably have taken place beyond the dock wall in the centre of the picture.

was unwilling to budge and the Navy Board, for their part, refused to renegotiate. A suspension of all the improvements going on at Milford was immediately ordered.

Two ships were still on the stocks, the 74-gunned *Portsmouth* and *Rochefort*, under the direction of French-born builder Louis Barrallier from Toulon. He was allowed to continue the work but the Navy Board was adamant, they would not be held to ransom by Greville and in the weeks and months ahead they would look elsewhere for their new dockyard.

They did not have to look far. The government already owned land further upstream, at Paterchurch Point, the location of the partly completed fort of 1759. When the area was surveyed by William Stone, Master Shipwright at the Milford yards, and John Rennie in the autumn of 1810 they found a low, flat, sheltered shelf of land with relatively deep water close inshore. It was the ideal place for a dockyard, they thought, and notice to quit the Milford yards was promptly given to Robert Fulke Greville on 2 August 1811. [3]

Charles Greville had once thought about building a harbour and dock at Paterchurch Point and even got as far as gathering together stones and other building material. The idea went no further and when the officers and men of the Navy Board arrived to mark out the new dockyard in 1812, all that broke the line of hills on the southern shore of the Cleddau River were the squat outline of the partially built fort and the ruins of an abandoned tower and mansion house known then as Paterchurch Tower.

There was certainly more space at Pater, as the area was called, but one great drawback was that there was no infrastructure to support the workforce, most of whom lived six miles downstream at Milford. Until houses could be built around the new yards the workers would have to travel every day, many of them rowing up and down the Haven at the beginning and end of every shift.

An old frigate, the *Lapwing*, was run ashore to act as temporary accommodation for the officers and the new enterprise began with the laying down of the keels of two 28-gun frigates, the *Ariadne* and the *Valorous*. These sixth rates, as they were known, were soon joined on the slipways by a further two frigates and, already looming large under the Pembrokeshire sun, a massive 74-gun ship of the line.

The dock before it became Pembroke Dock. The area, then known as Paterchurch, consisted of rolling meadowland and steep hills.

Pembroke Dockyard in the early days, few buildings and stockpiles of timber. Paterchurch Tower and mansion can be seen in the centre of this rather primitive painting by an unknown artist.

There was clearly an air of excitement and expectancy but, amazingly, the new yards began life without royal approval. There had been no Order in Council authorising the creation of the dockyard and shipbuilding had already begun when the request was formally made:

We beg leave to recommend ... that your Royal Highness will be graciously pleased to establish, by Your Order in Council, the yard forming at Pater as a Royal Dockyard.

The Navy Board of the Admiralty did, rather reluctantly, admit that it had begun operations in the Pembroke/Pater area, going on to declare that:

It will be necessary to appoint officers and clerks, many of whom we have found it necessary to appoint provisionally for the purpose of superintending the building of a 74-gun ship, two 5th and two 6th rates now building there.[4]

Prince George, then acting as Regent due to the insanity of his father, duly signed the Order on 31 October 1815, thus giving royal assent to the establishing of something that had already been operating for over twelve months.

The original dockyard covered an area of just twenty acres and it quickly became clear that more land was needed. This was bought from local landowners such as the Adams, Owens, and Meyrick families and slowly but inexorably the dockyard began to grow in size.

On 17 April 1814 the *Rochefort* was finally launched from Milford. Barrallier's work was over and the full establishment transferred to the new dockyard at Pater or Pembroke Dock as it became known. By Christmas 1814 there were 341 men employed in the yards, working as shipwrights and other related trades, while the Master Shipwright was Mr T. Roberts. It was, really, the beginning of the dockyard's 112 year history of shipbuilding – and of the town of Pembroke Dock.

The growth of Pembroke Dockyard throughout the first fifty years of the nineteenth century remains an amazing achievement. After the end of the Napoleonic Wars, the

The dockyard takes shape. This view from Llanion Point, *c.* 1817, shows one building shed already in operation and the first houses for dockyard workers stretching away to the east.

Royal Navy, understandably, entered a period of decline In 1815 there were 713 ships in commission but by the end of 1820 this figure had fallen to just 134 – two years earlier it had been as low as 121. The numbers of sailors was cut just as dramatically, manpower dropping from 140,000 in 1815 to 23,000 in 1820.[5]

Yet despite these huge reductions Pembroke Dockyard somehow seemed to 'buck the trend'. From the beginning, from the moment of its first two launches, it grew and continued to grow. By 1830 over 500 men were employed and when, in 1832, the Navy Board and the Admiralty Board were combined into one organisation as the Board of the Admiralty, Naval Officers were appointed to take charge of all Royal Dockyards.

Pembroke Dockyard, unlike most other royal yards which were run by an Admiral Superintendent, had only a Captain Superintendent in charge. It was a something that caused more than a little resentment over the years – but rarely from the Captain Superintendents themselves. They loved the tranquility and peace of the place. The first of the Captain Superintendents was Charles Bullen, CB, a Trafalgar veteran who was actually knighted during his tenure at Pembroke Dock. After leaving west Wales he went on to become an Admiral and died in 1853 at the ripe old age of eighty-six.

By 1850 Pembroke Dockyard had produced a wide range of ships, from huge woodenwalls to tiny cutters, from frigates and bomb ships to lighters and sloops. Nothing, it seemed, was beyond the skill of the Pembroke Dock workmen.

The quality of what was produced was even more remarkable when you consider that the dockyard did not have any decent fitting out facilities and so many of its ships were towed away to be completed elsewhere once they had been launched. Amazing as it may seem the cruiser *Essex*, launched in 1903, was the first vessel to be fully fitted out at Pembroke Dock.

The only things the dockyard seemed to have going for it were the close proximity of timber (the Forest of Dean) and, when the time came, of iron, thanks to the foundries at Landore. And yet the yards survived through many a crisis and, more than that, they prospered.

As in most other Royal Dockyards, the rate of production was variable and uneven. Some years the yards launched just one or two vessels while in others five or six ships went down the launching ways. In 1828, for example, six ships were launched, including the 46-gun *Hotspur*. In 1826 the figure was five, one of those being a simple lighter. In 1848 and 1852 just one ship was launched each year although, to be fair, the 1852 launch was that of the *Duke of Wellington*, the largest woodenwall ever built.

Launches normally took place in the spring and autumn, often to coincide with the high tides as it quickly became apparent that, despite first impressions, the water off the dockyard was not that deep and, unless dredged, it constantly silted up. Small vessels were sometimes launched two on the same tide; occasionally the second vessel went down the ways on the next tide on the same day.

But we are jumping ahead of ourselves. What is clear is that by 1816 it was already obvious that the dockyard was firmly established, the only Royal Naval yard in Wales and the only dockyard in Britain to be expanding in the wake of the Napoleonic Wars.

3

Early Ships

The first ships launched from Pembroke Dockyard were the 28-gun sixth rates or frigates *Ariadne* and *Valorous*. The *Ariadne* went into the water first, on the morning tide of 10 February 1816. She was launched bow first and was followed, later in the day, by her sister ship *Valorous*. This, the second ship built at the dockyard, entered the water stern first. Both vessels had been built on the same slip, stern to stern, both of them being laid down, constructed and launched in the open air.

Neither ship had a particularly distinguished career, the *Valorous* lasting barely thirteen years before being broken up at Chatham in 1829. She was the second ship in the Navy to bear the name *Valorous*, another and more distinguished vessel of the same name succeeding her in 1851.

The *Ariadne* served in various parts of the world but was perhaps most notable for being the last sea-going command of Captain Frederick Marryat, the author of well-known children's books such as *Mr Midshipman Easy* and *Masterman Ready*. Marryat had joined the Navy in 1806, in time to just miss Trafalgar, the greatest sea battle of the age. He did manage to win the Royal Humane Society Gold Medal for bravery, however, and took command of the *Ariadne* on 10 November 1828. Marryat's second novel, *The King's Own*, was actually written in the captain's cabin of the *Ariadne*. Clearly, the skipper already had literary aspirations.

The *Ariadne*, Pembroke Dock's first warship, finished her days as a coal hulk in Alexandria once she was paid off from her final cruise in 1837 and four years later, in 1841, was sold out of the Navy. By then Marryat had gone on to greater things and the technological developments of the early Victorian Age had made the *Ariadne* totally obsolete.

All of the early building work at Pembroke Dockyard was done in the open air. Conditions must have been hard as the workmen would have been exposed to the elements all day long. Often they were up to their knees, even their waists, in freezing water and mud.

The first ship to be built under cover, in a properly constructed building shed, was the diminutive cutter *Racer*. This covered slipway or building shed was soon added to and eventually the yards were able to boast no fewer than thirteen covered

This postcard, produced in 1914 to mark the centenary of the town and yards shows several Pembroke Dock ships. The two woodenwalls in the centre, alongside the Centenary Monument, were supposed to represent the *Ariadne* and *Valorous*, the first ships launched in 1816. In fact they are vessels much larger than a pair of 20-gun frigates.

building slips, more than any other dockyard in the country. But this came later when Pembroke Dockyard had established its reputation as a yard of unrivalled quality.

Measuring just sixty-three and a half feet in length, the little *Racer* was the fifth ship launched from the dockyard. She was comfortable to sail and reasonably well armed, at least for the job she had to do, being provided with two 6-pdr and four 6-pdr carronades. Like all cutters she was a single masted, square topsail vessel, fast and highly maneuverable.

Despite her obvious qualities, the *Racer* had a relatively short service life, as did many of the navy cutters at that time. Launched in 1818, she lasted just five years. She was sold out of the navy in 1823 and subsequently disappeared from view.

Every naval power employed cutters, their heyday being the hundred years between 1750 and 1850. Their duties were many and varied, from anti-pirate operations to mail carrying and reconnaissance. Their name was derived from their original use, the 'cutting out' or capture of enemy ships. In the naval campaigns of the seventeenth and eighteenth centuries these tiny vessels would carry parties of heavily armed sailors to moored or anchored enemy ships, which were then boarded and taken by storm. The captured ships, suitably 'cut out', would then be sailed back to the fleet.

Cutting out was a risky and dangerous procedure where speed and surprise were the essential elements but it was often preferable to unleashing a full broadside against the enemy. In any fleet action the damage inflicted on enemy ships was immense and the result was often an opponent who was sunk or damaged beyond repair. Cutting out would guarantee a captured prize – as long as it was done properly. As C. S. Forester wrote about one cutting out expedition involving his fictional character Hornblower:

> At the same moment came a shout from the corvette's deck, and when the shout was repeated it was echoed a hundredfold from the boats rushing alongside. The yelling was lusty and prolonged, of set purpose. A sleeping enemy would be bewildered by the din, and the progress of the shouting would tell each boat crew of the extent of the success of the others.[6]

The tiny cutters, fast and with shallow draft, were ideal for coastal work and many of them were often used in anti-smuggling operations. The *Sprightly*, launched from the yards in the summer of 1818, was probably loaned to the revenue services for exactly that purpose and subsequently used in the English Channel. Opinions vary on this but certainly there is no record of the ship having any service in the Royal Navy. The Excise Officers, however, did use a cutter of the same name, a ship that was launched

A Royal Navy cutter off the coast of Wales. The *Racer*, fifth vessel launched from the yards, would have been similar in appearance.

the same year as the Pembroke Dock vessel. Little else is known and the interpretation is, at best, surmise.

Another cutter built in the yards, and one that was destined to lead a long and more than useful life, was the *Speedy*, launched on 28 June 1828. She saw active service around the British coast for some time before being sent to the Caribbean where she remained for the next twenty-five years. Here she was engaged in anti-slavery work and in generally 'flying the flag' for Britain. Her first captain – who held the post for just three months before being promoted – was Charles Freemantle who later became Admiral Sir Charles Howe Freemantle, commander-in-chief at Plymouth.

The *Speedy* returned to Britain in August 1853 when she was converted to a mooring lighter at Devonport and renamed *YC 11*. Unfortunately, she was seriously damaged by fire and was consequently broken up in 1866 after a service career of nearly forty years.

The dangerous nature of sea faring in the days of sail is shown in the fate of the third vessel launched from Pembroke Dockyard, the 46-gun frigate *Thetis*. Launched on 1 February 1817 she enjoyed an active and adventurous life, mainly on the West Indies and America Station. Then in 1830 she was wrecked on the coast of Brazil while carrying a huge cargo of gold coin and bullion. Most of the cargo was salvaged by the sloop *Lightning*, also built at Pembroke Dock, but the *Thetis* was abandoned as a total wreck.

The *Thetis* was known throughout the Navy as 'Tea Chest,' thanks to an unusual experiment when, in 1823, the Admiralty decided to halve the rum ration on the ship and see what effect it had. Such a move was understandable as episodes of drunkenness among sailors – many of whom saved up their daily grog ration in order to get thoroughly drunk on a Saturday night – were very common and were causing great concern to those in high office. Tea and cocoa were issued to the men of the *Thetis* every day as an alternative to the normal grog, hence the ship's nickname.

There were compensations for the deprivation. Two shillings a month were added to the sailors' pay and the meatless days that all ships endured every week (banyan as it was called) were also cut out. Banyan, the name being taken from the Hindu word for those who did not eat meat, was originally introduced in 1563, the aim being to make sailors eat fish on these days and so extend or develop a strong fishing fleet which, in turn, would provide sailors through the Press Gang in times of war.

The downside of the experiment – quite apart from the reduction of the one piece of comfort sailors enjoyed – was the sad fact that for months after the exercise began the men from the *Thetis* were regularly beaten up by other sailors whenever they went ashore. Sailors throughout the Navy were afraid that the *Thetis* men would be responsible for a permanent cut in the rum ration.

In a way they were. The Admiralty was pleased with the reduction of drunken behaviour, at least on board the one ship where the trial had been held. To many seamen, however, it was the thin end of the wedge, a point that seemed to be reinforced when in 1825 the rum ration was halved throughout the navy. Banyan was totally abolished, which gave some small comfort, and in 1850 the rum ration was halved again. The evening issue of grog was abolished at the same time. The daily issue of beer had also been suspended in 1831, more cause for griping by the sailors!

In the 1820s and 1830s Pembroke Dockyard produced a large number of wooden sloops, vessels that preceded gunboats as the workhorses of the Navy. Typical of these was the *Helena*, launched on 11 July 1843. She carried just sixteen guns and spent most of her active life in the West Indies and on the west coast of Africa where she was one of many ships engaged in anti-slavery work.

The work was constant and was rarely celebrated or acknowledged. But it was necessary. On 29 July 1844 the *Helena* overtook and captured the slaver *Uniao* while a year later, on 8 April 1845, she detained the slave dhow *Messuri Khey* and freed eighty-eight slaves, just two of the many actions in which the *Helena* was involved.

The *Constance*, a 50-gun frigate launched on 12 March 1846 had a very early baptism of fire. On her shakedown cruise to Valparaiso she ran into a hurricane but, despite winds and waves of mountainous proportions, she came through intact. Her captain, Sir Baldwin Wake Walker was later to comment:

Nothing could have exceeded the way she went over it, not even straining a rope yarn.

In 1848 a party of sailors from the *Constance*, including her Captain, joined a force of some 250 soldiers and marines in a dangerous mission from Fort Victoria in Canada to intimidate local Indians, one of the many tasks the crew of frigates and sloops had to carry out.

In 1862 *Constance* was converted to screw propulsion, the first Pembroke Dock ship to be fitted with compound steam engines, even though the work was carried out at Devonport. Interestingly, on 26 October 1867 the whole crew was quarantined after an outbreak of yellow fever on board, hardly the most enjoyable of forced breaks on a ship just 180 feet long. The *Constance* was eventually sold off in 1875.

Sometimes Pembroke Dockyard had to build vessels very quickly in order to satisfy an immediate demand. The gun vessel *Flying Fish*, launched in December 1855 and re-rated as a sloop in 1859, was one of these. She was designed to operate in the shallow waters of the Baltic during the Crimean War but the conflict ended before she could be gainfully employed. Built of inferior wood – speed in her construction was everything – the *Flying Fish* was soon in a poor state and was broken up in 1866. Only her twin funnels distinguished her from other British gunboats of the time.

The dockyard's first 'big gun' vessel was the *Belleisle*, launched on 26 April 1819. Carrying seventy-four guns she had been on the slip for several years, a process that allowed the ship's timbers to settle and weather. It was a common enough practice in the pre-iron days of ship construction, one of the reasons why Pembroke Dockyard had so many slipways. Ships were partially completed, then left to 'weather' in the wind, rain and sun for months or years while the workforce moved on to another ship on another slipway.

The *Belleisle* was the second vessel to carry the name, the first being the captured French third rate *Formidable* which was taken in 1795 and commissioned into the Royal Navy. The Pembroke Dock *Belleisle* served in the Mediterranean for many years before being brought back home in 1841 and converted into a troopship. In this

Imogene and *Andromache*, launched in 1831 and 1832, are shown here passing the Chinese gun batteries of Bocca Tigris during the Opium Wars.

capacity she sailed for China in December 1841. She took part in the Opium Wars and was still in China when the Treaty of Nankin was signed in 1842.

Following the end of the Opium Wars the *Belleisle* returned to Britain where, still in her troopship role, she was based at Devonport. Then in 1854 came another change of duty when all but six of her guns were removed and she was converted into a hospital ship for the Baltic Fleet during the Crimean War. It was a role she kept until she was finally broken up in 1872.

The *Belleisle* held her tag as Pembroke Dock's largest ship for only a few years until, on 27 July 1824, the 84-gun *Vengeance* was launched. Modelled on a captured French battleship, she was given the nickname 'The wind's eye liner' by sailors as she quickly proved herself to be the fastest vessel in the Mediterranean Fleet. A fully rigged sailing ship of 2,284 tons, she took part in the Crimean War, despite being virtually obsolete by then, and finished her days as a receiving ship.

The yard's first vessel to carry over 100 guns was the *Royal William*, a ship of the line launched on 2 April 1833. She was followed by the *Rodney*, a 92-gun second rate which slid into the waters of Milford Haven two months later after spending six years waiting on the stocks.

By the middle of the 1830s Pembroke Dockyard was firmly established as one of the navy's premier building yards. Over fifty ships of varying size had been launched, most of them sailing vessels that would not have looked out of place in Nelson's navy. However, things were already changing and new developments such as the use of steam were beginning to affect shipbuilding.

The yard's first steam ship, driven by paddles rather than screw, was the *Tartarus*, launched on 23 June 1834. With a displacement of only 523 tons, she had a wooden hull and was armed with just two 9-pdr guns.

The *Vengeance*, launched from the yards on 27 July 1825.

Pembroke Dockyard and the western end of the town in the 1830s – several covered building slips now and plenty of activity in the Haven.

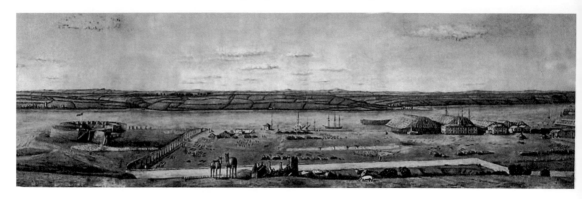

Pembroke Dockyard in about 1835. The covered building slips are taking shape and the huge dockyard wall around the establishment is already erected.

THE FERRY, PEMBROKE DOCK.

Hobbs Point slipway, always a ferry point for the people of Pembroke Dock as well as the fitting out berth for the yards, can be seen at the left of this print, *c.* 1861.

She served on the West Indies and North America Station between 1838 and 1841 but by 1856 she was based in the Mediterranean and was broken up at Malta in November 1860 after a fairly undistinguished career. Her claim to fame lay simply in the fact that she was Pembroke Dock's first steam-driven warship.

4

Woodenwalls

There is little doubt that Pembroke Dockyard produced some of the finest and best known of all wooden warships. Chief among these was the mighty *Duke of Wellington*.

Launched on 14 September 1852, she was originally called *Windsor Castle* but on the day of her launch news was received of the death of the Duke of Wellington, the much-lauded victor of the Battle of Waterloo and, more recently, a none too effective Prime Minister of Great Britain. On 1 October, within a few weeks of the ship's launch, she had been renamed *Duke of Wellington* in honour of the mighty Iron Duke.

The *Duke of Wellington* was originally designed by Sir William Symonds, Surveyor of the Navy, as a 140-gun ship of the line. Although ordered in 1841 she was not laid down until May 1849 when she was modified and altered by John Edye, Assistant to Symonds. Intended purely as a sailing vessel – the enormous paddle boxes needed for such a huge ship precluded the use of steam and would have limited the number of guns she could carry – it seemed to many that the *Duke of Wellington* was virtually obsolete even before she was launched.

The problem was solved by the introduction of screw propellers and when further modifications were made by Captain Baldwin Walker, who had replaced Symonds as Chief Surveyor, a crash programme was initiated in all RN Dockyards. In future, it was announced, the Royal Navy would be provided with an all-steam-driven battle fleet.

In a revolutionary process, the *Duke of Wellington* –*Windsor Castle* as she was still known at that stage – was cut in half while still on the stocks. The rear half of the ship was moved down the slipway, launched would not be an inappropriate word, and an extra 30 feet of length (giving the ship a new overall length of 270 feet) was added to the middle of the vessel. This allowed for engines to be fitted for the new screw propulsion which would now, along with her sails, drive the mighty warship. The engines, built by Robert Napier, had been intended for the frigate *Simoon* but the need of the new battleship, it was felt, was greater. The whole process of 'launching' the after section of the ship took only an hour and a half.

The *Duke of Wellington* was, not surprisingly, given a new figurehead once her name had been changed, a replica or representation of the Iron Duke himself. Carved from 70 cubic feet of timber, this massive showpiece was brought to Pembroke Dock

The launch of the *Duke of Wellington* – still called *Windsor Castle* until a few days later – on 14 September 1852. *The Duke of Wellington* was the largest woodenwall ever built.

The *James Watt* slides down the slipway in April 1853, the only ship in the Royal Navy to ever hold the name.

by the *Widgeon* while the steam frigate *Simoon*, whose engines she had purloined, brought the battleship's masts and rigging.

The *Duke of Wellington* was, briefly, the most powerful warship in the world. She served in the Channel Fleet and flew the flag of Sir Charles Napier in the Baltic during the Crimean War. She was undoubtedly a magnificent sailing ship, which was what she had originally been designed for, but her engines were hopelessly inadequate and her performance under steam was unsatisfactory.

Paid off after the Crimean War, she became a Guard Ship at Devonport and then, from 1863 onwards, she operated as the Receiving Ship for recruits at Portsmouth. With her huge oak hull dwarfing all other vessels in the harbour, for many years she was probably the most photographed ship in the Navy, operating as the flagship of the Port Admiral at Portsmouth between 1869 and 1891 – a role she inherited from Nelson's *Victory*.

The *Duke of Wellington* was also flagship of the Commander in Chief for a brief period and between 1900 and 1902 was commanded by no less a figure than David Beatty, future Admiral of the Fleet and commander of the battlecruiser squadron at the Battle of Jutland. Eventually, her timbers rotting and by now hopelessly out of date, the crew was moved ashore and the ship was sold for breaking in 1904.

The *Duke of Wellington* had a long and distinguished record of service. But she was not alone in that, other Pembroke Dock ships serving just as long.

The *Fisgard* – the old spelling of the Pembrokeshire town and port – was one. This 46-gun Lede-class frigate was launched on 8 July 1819 and spent sixty years as a Navy warship. She was built for a cost of £23,493 but spent the first twenty-four years of her life laid up, only coming into active service in 1843.

After commissioning, she was immediately sent to the Pacific where Fishguard Island and Duntze Head on the coast of Canada were named after her and her captain, John Duntze. On her return to Britain the *Fisgard* became harbour flagship at Woolwich before being, eventually, sold for breaking. She passed on her name, however, to a 'stone frigate,' a shore establishment training engineers and artificers.

The *Melampus*, launched in 1820, was another Pembroke Dock vessel with more than a little longevity. With a displacement of 1,089 tons, she was yet another 46-gun frigate of the Lede-Class, very much a 'Jack of all trades' in the early nineteenth century navy. She served in several different parts of the world, notably on the south east coast of America and in the East Indies.

In June 1856 she was lying at Constantinople when she received orders to return to Britain. Calling at Malta and Gibraltar, she was back in Sheerness by 21 August when she was paid off. This was not the end of her service life, however, as she was immediately commissioned as a Guard Ship, a role she carried out until 1857. Her career after that was in harbour service, mainly in the Portsmouth area, until, finally, on 3 April 1906 she was sold to a company by the name of Harris in the Bristol area. In all, the service life of the *Melampus* lasted for eighty-six years.

Another long serving woodenwall was the frigate *Andromache*, launched from the yards on 27 August 1832. One day in 1836 the ship was lying at anchor in Madras Roads. There was a heavy swell running and a fresh breeze blowing, but nevertheless Captain Henry Chads ordered his men to begin firing and target practice.

A whole broadside was dispatched at a buoy some 600 yards distant and virtually all of the shot fell close to or actually on the buoy. The full broadside was fired in one minute and twenty-five seconds. Broadsides were loosed off for over three minutes and the whole process of running out the cannon, firing and then securing for sea again took six minutes and fifty-nine seconds. It was an amazing performance, showing the strength and calibre of Royal Navy fire power – small wonder that in 1845 Henry Chads was appointed captain of HMS *Excellent*, the Naval gunnery school.

After twenty years' service across the world the *Andromache* became a powder hulk in 1854. She was broken up at Devonport in 1875.

Second careers, as powder hulks or lighters, once active service life was over, seem to have been a common occurrence for many ships at this time. And several of the Pembroke Dock vessels duly became training ships where men and boys could learn their trade as seafarers.

Most notable of these was the *Clarence*, launched from the yards on 25 July 1827 as an 84-gun second rate. With a displacement of 2,288 tons and a length of nearly 200 foot, she was the ideal size to be converted into a training ship and in 1872, her useful service life over, she was given on more or less permanent loan to the Liverpool branch of the Catholic Reformatory Association. She was towed to the Mersey and moored off Rock Ferry.

The aim of the Victorian Reformatory School Ships – three of them in all, moored on the Mersey and the Thames – was to provide delinquent boys with harsh discipline that might help them to give up their criminal lives and reform. If possible the Reformatory Ships would also place boys into jobs at sea once their terms of 'imprisonment' were over. The system was largely ineffective and unsuccessful, however, and very few of the trainees ever went to sea. Those who did usually managed just one voyage and then sought easier ways of making a living.

The *Clarence* was intended to take 250 Catholic boys but she was rarely full. Unlike her counterparts, however, she did at least have a reasonable record in sending a large proportion of her boys to sea. In 1888, for example, out of fifty-nine discharges, forty-one of them went to sea.[7]

Although successful in one respect, the behaviour of the *Clarence* boys was always a cause of concern to the Home Office Inspectors who had a duty to report on the conditions on board such ships. In 1882 a boy had been caught trying to set fire to the vessel while a few months later there was a mutiny on board that resulted in several youngsters being carted off to prison.[8]

Arsonists were more successful in 1884. On the afternoon of 17 January, about 1.30 p.m., a fire was discovered on the ship's lower deck. The seat of the fire was close to a hold where oil cans were stored and flames spread so quickly that crew and staff were beaten back when they tried to reach it. Within a very short space of time it was clear that the *Clarence* was doomed, flames shooting up thirty or forty feet into the air. Two Rock Ferry steamers came alongside and took off the boys.[9]

The following morning the fires were still raging. Attempts to destroy by cannon fire what was, by now, little more than a smoldering hulk met with failure, proof if any was needed of the strength of the old ship's timbers. Eventually she was rammed by a

Right: The figurehead of the *Hamadryad*, launched in July 1823 and later hospital ship at Cardiff for many years.

Below: The training ship *Clarence*, later destroyed in an arson attack by the trainees, is shown here in the River Mersey.

steamer and, after two attempts, the *Clarence* turned onto her side and sank beneath the waves. Seven boys from the ship were found guilty of arson and sent off to prison for five years.

The Catholic Reformatory Association immediately applied to the Admiralty for another vessel and, after some prevarication, the *Royal William* was offered. By pure chance she was another Pembroke Dock vessel, the first 100-plus gun ship produced by the yards and launched in 1833. Originally a first rate sailing ship of the line, she had spent most of her life in home waters and in 1860 was converted to screw propulsion. By 1884 she was laid up and out of service.

The Catholic Reformatory Association happily accepted the Admiralty's offer and their new Training Ship, now renamed *Clarence* in honour of the original ship, was moored in the Mersey in November 1885. Her induction as a training ship was far from easy as within months there was a mutiny on board, a mutiny that resulted in the Schoolmaster being stabbed. The uprising was only quelled when Captain Statham threatened the ringleaders with a pistol. It was, incidentally, a pistol for which he had no ammunition.

Unhappily, this ship, too, met an untimely end when, like her predecessor, she was destroyed by fire, this time on the night of 26 July 1899. Bishop Allen of Shrewsbury was aboard at the time as he had come to confirm several boys the following day but he and all of the trainees were safely evacuated. Once again, it was clear that the fire was too fierce to be extinguished and the *Clarence/Royal William* was abandoned.

Boys in training on the deck of the *Royal William*, rechristened *Clarence* after the first ship of the name was destroyed by fire in 1884.

At 6.00 a.m. the next morning, just four hours after the fire had broken out, the ship broke in two. One half sank quickly, the other half 'remaining afloat for some time, a mass of burning wood and spars.'[10] Although it was originally thought to be an accident it quickly transpired that a small group of boys had been planning the arson attack for some time and had built up a store of wood and rags in the bowels of the vessel.

With two Pembroke Dock ships condemned to a watery grave the Catholic Reformatory Association decided to cut their losses and thereafter transferred their nautical training to a land-based school near Widnes.

The *Arethusa* of 1849 was yet another Pembroke Dock vessel converted into a training ship, this time for one of the most famous of all Victorian charities, the Shaftesbury Society. The Society had been founded by the Earl of Shaftesbury and a disabled clerk by the name of William Williams in the early days of the new Queen's reign. The charity operated for several years in and around the Home Counties area. Then, on the evening of 14 February 1866, over 150 vagrant and destitute boys answered the Earl's invitation to a supper at St Giles Refuge in London. The Earl proposed obtaining a ship and starting a training school on board. Would they be interested? The answer was a resounding 'Yes.'

The Society's first vessel was the tiny *Chichester* but it was not long before a bigger and larger ship was needed. As a consequence, in 1874 the Pembroke Dock built *Arethusa* was brought to Greenhithe and began her new role as a Nautical Training School.

Launched on 20 June 1849, the fifty gun frigate *Arethusa* was one of the last all-wooden warships of the Royal Navy to go into action. She fought in the Crimean War, at the Battles of Odessa and Sevastapol, and was converted to a screw frigate in 1861. When the Earl of Shaftesbury approached the Admiralty about the possibility of being loaned a new vessel, she was nearing the end of her active life and, with no other prospect of use, the old ship was promptly offered and accepted.

Life on the *Arethusa* was both spartan and hard. Boys were not given boots until they had spent six months on board when, it was felt, they would be less likely to run away. And the food was nothing if not basic. Breakfast, for example, consisted of half a roll of bread and a basin of cocoa; dinner was simply a few pieces of scorched mutton with boiled potatoes. But it was certainly a lot better than any of the boys would have enjoyed on the streets of London.[11]

The *Arethusa* continued as a training ship until 1932. By this time she was old and in very poor condition. The Society replaced her with a four-masted German barque called the *Peking* and despite lying alongside the new vessel for a few years, by 1934 it was clear that the end of the original ship had come. The *Arethusa* was sold off and duly broken up while the *Peking*, now renamed *Arethusa*, was moved to Upnor on the Medway. The figurehead of the old ship was placed on the river bank at Upnor as a memorial to her many years of service to the Society.

The new *Arethusa* ran as the Shaftesbury Society's training ship for many years and now acts as a museum at South Street Sea Port in New York, under her original name of *Peking*.

The *Arethusa* waiting to be towed away for breaking, *c.* 1934. Note, the ship's figurehead has already been removed and placed on the river bank at Upnor where the *Arethusa* was moored for nearly fifty years.

The Royal Navy did not just loan vessels out to charities. Often they used obsolete ships themselves as training vessels and several Pembroke Dock ships ended their working lives this way.

The frigate *Inconstant*, launched in 1868 – along with her two sister ships, the last Royal Navy ship to be designated 'frigate' until the name was revived for anti-submarine vessels during the Second World War – was one such. As a training ship she was at various times known as *Impregnable II*, *Defiance IV* and *Defiance II* and was a part of the Torpedo School in the Hamoaze. When she was broken up in April 1956 the *Inconstant* had the honour of being the last Pembroke Dock vessel still afloat.

The *Defiance*, launched in 1861, was a second rate battleship that became the main ship in the Plymouth Torpedo School in November 1884. She was sold for breaking in 1931 but her name lived on as far as the establishment was concerned. The *Defiance* was joined by the protected cruiser *Andromeda*, launched from the dockyard in 1898 and converted to a training ship under the name *Powerful* in 1913.

The *Howe*, launched from Pembroke Dockyard in 1860 as one of the last three-decker battleships ever built for the Royal Navy, also became a training school, replacing the *Impregnable* and taking her name in September 1886. The *Impregnable* had also been launched in 1860 – although not from Pembroke Dock – and was, thanks to the *Warrior*, obsolete even as she hit the water. She made only one cruise before being mothballed in the Hamoaze and then converted into a training ship. By

The battleship *Howe*, launched at Pembroke Dock in 1860, which replaced the *Impregnable* (and took her name) as a Royal Navy training ship on the Hamoaze.

Another view of the *Howe*, as a training ship, this time dressed overall for Queen Victoria's Diamond Jubilee.

1918, just before it was paid off, the 'Impregnable group' included the *Emerald*, *Black Prince* and *Inconstant* – and, of course, the *Howe/Impregnable*.

In 1869 the 110-gun *Windsor Castle* replaced the *Cambridge* as the Gunnery Training Ship at Portsmouth, her name being changed as tradition demanded to

The *Lion*, fully rigged and moored off Torpoint – she was connected to the *Implacable* by a gangway.

that of the original ship. The *Windsor Castle* had spent fourteen years on the stocks at Pembroke Dock and even after her launch was never fitted out for sea. She had been laid down as the *Victoria* so the change of name to *Cambridge* was not entirely unexpected. She was finally sold for breaking in 1908.

The *Lion*, launched from Pembroke Dockyard on 29 July 1847 as an 80-gun second rate, became a boys training ship in 1871, lying moored to the *Implacable* in the Hamaoze at Devonport. The *Implacable* was originally the French battleship *Duguay Trouin* which had fought at Trafalgar and while she had most of her masts removed, the *Lion* was left with masts and spars intact so that trainees could carry out drill aloft. A gangway connected the two ships which were moored stern to stern.

The *Lion* became infamous as, in common with other Royal Navy training ships, she refused to take boys who had criminal records. Arthur Byron was sent to the *Lion* after several years on the Industrial Training Ship *Clio*, then moored in the Menai Straits. He was doing well, receiving nothing but excellent reports. Then some long forgotten criminal offence came to light and Byron was immediately discharged from the ship. There was no appeal.

Pembroke Dock was a dockyard created to build wooden warships. It was a task the workers carried out with great skill. They were proud of their abilities, rightly so, but in the middle years of the nineteenth century few of them could even begin to realise the difficulties that lay ahead.

5

Ghosts, Churches and Hospitals

Sailors have always been superstitious individuals and the stories of ghosts and weird happenings on board ship are legendary.

The best known ghost story involving the town and dockyard at Pembroke Dock is that of the ghost and HMS *Asp*. The *Asp* was not a Pembroke Dock ship but many of the hauntings in the tale took place in the dockyard when she called in for repair or refitting. Her commander, Captain Aldridge, wrote a letter to *The Pembroke County Guardian* on 15 September 1869, describing in some detail the events as he remembered them.

Aldridge took over the *Asp* as she was undergoing repairs at Pembroke Dock. Almost immediately, he was approached by the Captain Superintendent of the yard, informing him that the ship was said to be haunted and that most of the dockyard men were refusing to work on her. At the time Aldridge thought nothing of the claim and dismissed it as mere sailors' superstition.

Over the next few months, however, as the *Asp* sailed around the coast in her duties as a survey vessel, strange noises – drawers being opened and shut, the click of a percussion cap being snapped alongside the captain's head as he slept – became commonplace. Then came something a little more sinister, as Captain Aldridge wrote:

> One night, when the vessel was at anchor, I was woken by the quartermaster begging me to come on deck as the look-out man had rushed to the lower deck, saying that a figure of a lady was standing on the paddle box pointing with her finger to Heaven.[12]

Aldridge could see nothing and when the look-out was ordered back on watch he immediately went into convulsions. The captain himself was forced to carry out the remainder of the duty. In the weeks following that first appearance, the apparition, always with its finger raised to the sky, was seen many times and several crew members ran screaming from the ship. Nothing the captain could say or do would convince them to return.

The ghost and the *Asp*, artist's impression.

Events reached their climax when the *Asp* once more put into Pembroke Dockyard in 1857. On the first evening of the refit the ship was moored to the wall alongside one of the slipways. All was quiet and calm until a sentry on the dockside suddenly saw the shape of a lady mount the inshore paddle box and point to the sky:

> She then stepped ashore and came along the path towards him when he brought his musket to the charge. 'Who goes there?' But the figure walked through the musket, upon which he dropped it and ran for the guardhouse.[13]

Other soldiers also claimed to see the apparition that night and one of them even discharged his musket. But the figure simply glided on until it reached the ruins of the old Paterchurch Tower. And there it stood, finger raised to the Heavens until it suddenly disappeared. That was the last sighting of the *Asp*'s ghost. It was later claimed that the *Asp* had once run mail between Port Patrick and Donaghadee in Ireland and during this time the body of a young woman had been discovered in the aft cabin, her throat cut open from ear to ear.

Whether or not Captain Aldridge had allowed time and old age to affect his recollections – his letter was not written and published until thirty years after the supposed hauntings – or whether he was taking a mischievous poke at the superstitions of sailors and dockyard workers will never be known. And then again, maybe, just maybe, there might be some substance in the old legend. Whatever the explanation, the story has gone down in the folklore of Pembroke Dock.

The frigate *Inconstant* had a career that took her all over the world before finishing as a training ship at Devonport. It has been claimed that on 11 July 1881 Prince

The *Inconstant*– centre of the three ships. A future king swore he saw a phantom ghost ship from her decks!

George, the future King George V, saw a phantom ship from her deck while he was serving on board.

George, along with his brother Eddy, were serving Royal Naval officers engaged in a two year, round the world cruise on board the sloop *Bacchante*, visiting places such as South America, South Africa and Australia. Unfortunately, the *Bacchante* damaged her rudder in a heavy sea and had to put into port for repair. Prince George was forced to transfer to the *Inconstant* while the repairs were being carried out.

Sailing between Melbourne and Sydney, in company with the *Tourmaline* and *Cleopatra*, several men on the *Inconstant* also saw the phantom ship and informed their superior officers. The sighting was never explained but Prince George was adamant – he had seen the phantom or ghost ship sailing alongside the tiny fleet.

Some ships were simply regarded as unlucky. One of these was the wooden paddle frigate *Gorgon*, launched on Thursday 31 August 1837. Together with her sister ship *Cyclops* – similar in style and armament but twelve feet shorter – the two ships were the navy's first steam vessels over 1,000 tons. As such they were revolutionary vessels.

The Captain Superintendent of the yards at the time was William Pryce Cumby, a veteran and hero of the Battle of Trafalgar, taking over command of the *Bellerophon* when her Captain was killed. He had been in charge at Pembroke Dockyard for just a few months and was more than pleased when it was decided that his wife should have the honour of christening the new ship.[14]

Unfortunately, Cumby was taken ill that same night and never recovered his health. He died on 27 September on board the old Royal Yacht *Royal Sovereign* which was acting as his accommodation. All dockyard maties and sailors shuddered when they heard the news. It just reinforced what they already felt about the ship. She was unlucky and if Cumby's death was not proof enough, they said, try spelling her name backwards – horror of horrors, it read 'No Grog'.

The launch of the battleship *Caesar*, supposedly on 21 July 1853, was another occasion when rumours of witchcraft and sorcery were rife in the town. The occasion was imbued with all the pomp and ceremony demanded in the launching of a 90-gun man of war but when the moment came, the *Caesar* stuck fast. No matter what the officials could say, no matter what the dockyard workers tried to do, the ship refused to be launched.

For the people of Pembroke Dock, thousands of whom had poured into the yards to watch the launch, as custom allowed, the failure was down to one person, the local witch Betty Foggy. She, too, had tried to gain admission to the yards but had been turned away because, it was felt, her presence would be unlucky. As she tottered off down the street she was heard to mutter 'Very well, if I can't come in there will be no launch today.'

The news spread like wildfire. 'Betty's cursed the launch!' In fact the failure was down to two things. Firstly, someone had ordered fir – a soft wood – to be used instead of oak on the launching ways and, secondly, the tallow used to grease those ways was decidedly inferior. The result? As she was built, and as she became heavier and heavier, the *Caesar* simply bedded herself into the wood.

The battleship *Caesar* – rumours of witchcraft and sorcery surrounded her launch – is shown here in a print from *The Illustrated London News*.

It was Sunday 7 August, with the people of the town conveniently at morning service, before the *Caesar* was finally launched. For over two weeks workmen had toiled ceaselessly, building huge wooden camels beneath her hull to raise the ship out of the wood. But, to everyone in Pembroke Dock, it was a simple matter. Betty Foggy had lifted her curse. Quite what Betty thought as the *Caesar* was towed away by the *Magicienne* to be fitted out at Portsmouth will never be known but, for a brief while at least, she surely relished and revelled in her notoriety.

At the other end of the spectrum, several Pembroke Dock vessels finished their days as church ships. Principal amongst these was the *Thisbe*, launched from the yards on 9 September 1824.

In 1835 Anglican clergyman John Ashley began a regular ministry for the farmers and fishermen on Flat and Steep Holm Islands in the Bristol Channel. Sailing in a small hired boat, an open decked vessel that invariably left him drenched, shivering and nearly drowned, he also regularly ventured out to the ships moored in Penarth Roads, waiting to enter Cardiff Docks. It was the beginning of an organisation that soon became known as the Bristol Channel Mission, offering solace and Christian comfort to sailors and lighthouse keepers in the Channel.[15]

In 1858 the organisation became a national body, the Missions to Seamen, and Ashley asked the Admiralty for the loan of a ship on which he could establish and run a permanent church. They gave him the *Thisbe*. The fifth rate frigate had spent most of her service life in the Plymouth and Devonport area and was ready to be broken up when the request arrived.

She sailed into Cardiff in late 1863 and was moored in East Bute Dock, a church soon being erected on her quarterdeck. Under the leadership of the Superintendent,

The frigate *Thisbe*, launched from the dockyard in September 1824, is shown here in her later role as church or gospel ship in Cardiff docks.

Mr Gale, services were held every Tuesday, Friday and Sunday, sometimes as many as 600 people – sailors, their wives, pilots and even people from the immediate area – crowding onto the decks of the old ship.

It wasn't just religious services on offer. Newspapers were provided, around 100 people using the 'reading room' every day. There was a small library and paper, ink and pens were also available. In 1877 alone some 4,000 letters were posted in the box on board the *Thisbe*. Magic lantern shows were held several evenings each week and every Thursday there was a 'concert entertainment' or the singing of sacred songs. Games tournaments took place at 5.00 p.m. every Wednesday.

Mr Gale was hugely effective in his work and the number of conversions in the docks area of Cardiff increased dramatically. The ship was old, however, and by the early 1890s the congregation had outgrown the facilities. Mr Gale had no option but to leave the *Thisbe* and found a church on land. Eventually this became Ebenezer Church while the *Thisbe* was sold and scrapped in 1892.

The *Hotspur*, an 1828 Seringapatam-Class frigate, was another vessel to become a church ship. She did not see much service and was actually laid up, incomplete, at Portsmouth for many years. By 1859 she was operating as a chapel hulk at Devonport but in 1865 was converted into a Roman Catholic Chapel Ship. By now she had been renamed *Monmouth* and served in this capacity until a Catholic Church was opened in nearby Keyham.

The *Helena* of 1843 had several different roles in her long life. After many years on anti-slavery patrols in the West Indies and off the west African coast, in 1861 she became a coal hulk at Portsmouth. Two years later she was converted to a police hulk and then, in 1868, she was taken to Ipswich where she became a floating chapel. She remained in this role until 1883, thousands of sailors passing over her decks each Sunday, until she reverted to her police duties, this time at Chatham. The *Helena* was only finally broken up in 1921.

One of the strangest of all stories with a religious interest concerned the *Thetis*, the famous 'Tea Chest,' launched from the yards in 1817. In 1824 she called at St Michaels in the Azores where her captain was immediately visited by a delegation from the island's Anglican community. They wanted the *Thetis* to carry a message to the Archbishop of Canterbury, requesting him to appoint a Bishop to the island in order to consecrate their new cemetery.

Ever the pragmatist, the captain of the *Thetis*, realising it would be many months before he could get a message to the Archbishop, simply appointed his chaplain to the office. The ship's writer prepared a warrant confirming the chaplain as Bishop of St Michaels and the consecration ceremony was duly carried out. Thereupon the chaplain reverted to his normal role and the *Thetis* sailed away. It is a piece of ecclesiastical history that is rarely remembered. Quite what the Church authorities thought about the actions of the Captain is not recorded either.

Hospitals or any means of caring for sick sailors always presented something of a problem to the Admiralty. The Hospital of St Bartholomew in Sandwich appears to have been the first medical establishment created just for sailors, closely followed by a twelve-bed unit in Bristol, founded in 1445. These, however, and one or two others

The *Thetis* – a bishop among her crew and grog reduced by half before being wrecked off the coast of Brazil. An adventurous life, indeed.

like them, largely disappeared following Henry VIII's Dissolution of the Monasteries in the 1530s and for many years any kind of medical provision for sailors – or for the general public for that matter – was very much on an ad hoc basis.

As towns and cities grew, so the need for proper medical services grew with them. Thanks to the booming coal trade, in the early and middle years of the nineteenth century Cardiff had developed into the most important port in Britain. Hundreds of sailors flooded into the port every week and it soon became apparent that they could be bringing infectious diseases with them.

The Hamadryad Hospital was the brainchild of Dr Henry Paine, Medical Officer of Health for Cardiff between 1855 and 1887. He was frightened that diseases such as smallpox, cholera and typhoid might be brought into the city by sailors and passed on to the residents. And so he suggested a Seaman's Hospital, close to the docks but far enough away from the city houses to prevent the spread of disease. Such an enterprise, Paine believed, could be paid for by a levy on shipping agents and on the owners of the vessels using the docks.

At a public meeting in March 1866 it was agreed that a hospital ship should be established. The Admiralty was approached and they agreed to loan the old Leda-Class frigate *Hamadryad*.

The *Hamadryad* had been launched from Pembroke Dockyard on 25 June 1823, the fifteenth ship built in the yards. At 152 feet in length (beam measurement being 40½ feet) she was certainly not big and, having been laid up at Devonport ready for breaking, she was also decidedly old. But she was all that was available. Her naval career had been uneventful, the ship never having been in action, but now she was prepared to take on the biggest challenge she would ever face.

Taken to Cardiff, the *Hamadryad* was fitted out as a hospital ship for a total cost of £2,791 – including a charge of £160 for towing her from Devonport. Initially she was moored in East Bute Dock but she was soon moved to a piece of waste ground (given by the Marquis of Bute) known by the unappealing name of Rat Island. And here she lay from 1 November 1866 until 1905.

The *Hamadryad* took patients from the port of Cardiff and also from Swansea, Barry and Newport docks, as well as local people should the need arise. In the first year alone there were over 400 admissions and by 1871 the demand was so great that a wooden annexe had to be built close by on the river bank. An 1897 report from Dr Hughes, the Medical Superintendent, stated that 379 people had been treated as 'in patients' that year, many more being given assistance as day patients. Of those admitted, seventeen had died, nine of them from natural causes, the others because of the accidents that had injured them in the first place.[16]

Patients, as might be expected in a place like Cardiff, came from all over the world and dozens of nationalities were helped on the *Hamadryad*. No women were admitted or treated – and nobody suffering from lice or scabies either. After admission all patients were given a bath and a haircut, then issued with a set of hospital clothes, a procedure that continued into the twentieth century.

The *Hamadryad* was funded by a levy of two shillings per 100 tons of registered shipping in Cardiff Docks and was collected either from the ships' captains themselves or from shipping agents at the Dock Office.

Eventually, in order to celebrate the Diamond Jubilee of Queen Victoria in 1897 it was decided to build a permanent Seaman's Hospital close to the original site. This

The *Hamadryad* is shown here in her last days, operating as the hospital ship in Cardiff docks.

The *Druid* of 1827, shown here on a postage stamp for St Kitts.

was opened on 29 June 1905, the hospital continuing its work until 2002, and the *Hamadryad* was suddenly surplus to requirements once again. Many tons of pig iron and stone ballast was removed from her hull before she was floated off her mudbank, taken down a specially prepared channel and towed to Appledore for breaking up.

The *Belleisle* was another Pembroke Dock vessel to act as a hospital ship. This was during the Crimean War, the conversion having taken place in 1854. The role continued after peace was signed with the *Belleisle* serving at both Chatham and Sheerness. The 46-gun frigate *Nerius*, launched on 30 July 1821 as one of the earliest Pembroke Dock ships, became a hospital ship at Plymouth. It was a role she occupied until 1842, before being taken to Valparaiso as a store depot ship. She was finally being sold out of the navy in 1879.

The *Druid*, launched as a 46-gun frigate on 1 July 1825, served in China during the Opium Wars between 1839 and 1842. She was heavily involved in the operations that led to the capture of Canton in May 1841 as well as the destruction of the Chinese admiral's flagship *Cambridge*. Twelve of her crew and two Royal Marines were killed during these campaigns.

In 1846 the *Druid* returned to Britain and was hulked. A further role for her was found, however, as she was soon moved to Liverpool where she became a lazaretto, a hospital ship for sailors with infectious diseases. It was a role she occupied for several years before being sold in April 1863 and broken up at Plymouth.

Churches, chapels and hospitals – as well as stories of witchcraft and hauntings – all part of the daily life of Pembroke Dock's ships.

6

Royal Yachts

By the middle years of the nineteenth century Pembroke Dockyard had acquired for itself a significant reputation for the building of wooden warships. So it was no surprise when the order came through to build a Royal Yacht for Queen Victoria.

Many of Britain's monarchs had used Royal Yachts down the centuries, vessels that would take them on official business around the coast. In the days when roads were poor or even non-existent, travel by boat was both easy and relatively safe. It wasn't all plain sailing, however. Henry V once sold off all Royal Yachts in order to clear the monarchy's debts and, of course, to fund the inevitable wars with France. Not until the reign of Henry VIII did Royal Yachts reappear on the scene.

The pleasure loving Charles II had twenty-five Royal Yachts during his reign. Admittedly, some of these were no more than small river craft but by the time Victoria succeeded to the throne in June 1837 there were still five of them in service. On her accession Victoria was able to use the *Royal Adelaide* but this was not the most suitable or comfortable of vessels and, in due course, she petitioned Parliament for a new yacht. After some discussion this was agreed.

Designed by Sir William Symonds, the *Victoria and Albert* (I) was launched from Pembroke Dockyard on 26 April 1843. She was the first Royal Yacht to be steam powered and at 225 feet in length, 33 feet in the beam, she was small in stature but still large enough to provide a degree of comfort for the Royal family.

The operative word is 'degree'. Victoria herself wrote in her journal on 23 September 1843 about the first voyage she and Albert made in the new vessel – 'Woke rather early, there being nothing as proper curtains to keep out the light.' Such lack of comfort probably quite suited the aloof and spartan Prince Albert; Victoria would obviously have preferred something a little more decorous.

The Royal Yachts were never intended for long distance sailing; they were purely for cruises around the coast of Britain and, occasionally, for trips across to the continent. If any cruise was planned to more distant parts then a liner (such as the *Ophir* which took the Duke and Duchess of York around the British Empire in 1901) or one of the big gun battleships of the fleet would be used.

The Queen's first Pembroke Dock yacht *Victoria and Albert* (I) bids farewell to the *Duke of Wellington* and Admiral Napier's Baltic Fleet in Spithead, 1854.

Nevertheless, Victoria and her consort enjoyed many a happy time on the *Victoria and Albert*, over twenty separate voyages being made. Together with the tender *Fairy* they would cruise along the south coast, stopping whenever they saw an attractive cove or harbour. As *The Times* wrote in September 1846:

> Her Majesty, with the steamer squadron, on Saturday proceeded to Mount's Bay, and there remained until yesterday ... Yesterday afternoon the squadron got under weigh (sic) and returned to this port as previously arranged, and it is said en voyage the Queen, Prince and two children, accompanied by Mr Taylor of the Duchy Office, landed on the beach at Kynance Cove, a locality near the Lizard, much celebrated in Cornish history for its local features and romantic attraction, and remained there for some time picking up shells and other natural curiosities.[17]

These were holiday excursions for the royal family, of course, but there were also state occasions that demanded considerably more pomp and ceremony. And it was not long before the *Victoria and Albert* (I) was considered to be far too small and somewhat lacking in gravitas. Consequently, a new Royal Yacht was ordered from the yards at Pembroke Dock. This vessel was also to be known as the *Victoria and Albert*.

The new yacht was launched on 16 January 1855. Like all Royal Yachts she was owned and operated by the Royal Navy, 240 sailors being posted to the ship as soon as she came into service. On 22 December 1854 the first *V and A* had been renamed *Osborne* to allow the *Victoria and Albert* (II) to come into the world and under this new name she continued to offer service to the royal family until she was finally scrapped in 1868.

The launch of the second *Victoria and Albert* at Pembroke Dockyard, 16 January 1855. Huge celebrations greeted the event.

The Royal Yacht *Osborne*, built originally for the Prince of Wales. He hated the vessel, Victoria loved her and used her whenever she could.

A sad but inevitable end for most ships. The Royal Yacht *Osborne* lies, disused and ready for breaking, at Felixstowe.

The *Victoria and Albert* (II) measured 360 feet in length and with her two steam-driven paddles could make 15 knots in a moderate sea. She was considerably more ornate than the original vessel and remained the principal Royal Yacht until 1900 when she was replaced by yet another *V and A*.

There were other royal vessels during these years, however, all built at Pembroke Dockyard.

The *Osborne*, named after Victoria's house on the Isle of Wight, was launched on 19 December 1870. Interestingly, she was originally built for Edward, Prince of Wales, but as he detested the house on the Isle of Wight it was perhaps understandable that she was not exactly his favourite vessel. She did, however, become a great favourite of the Queen.

Designed by Sir Edward Reed, she was a paddle yacht of 1,856 tons and was 100 feet shorter than the *V and A* (II) which gave her a more personal feel. Victoria preferred making state trips abroad on this ship than on the official Royal Yacht, the *Victoria and Albert* (II). Bertie, more concerned with the pleasure dens of the West End, did not object. The *Osborne* was finally decommissioned in 1908 and scrapped soon afterwards.

Perhaps Victoria's favourite yacht of all was the *Alberta*, launched on 3 October 1863. Never officially a Royal Yacht, she was designated Passage Boat or tender, replacing the *Fairy*, which finally went to the breakers yard that same year. A tiny vessel, just 160 feet long, Queen Victoria loved the *Alberta* right from the start. Yet it was a relationship that was not without difficulties.

On 18 August 1875, with the Queen on board, the *Alberta* was in collision with a private yacht, the *Mistletoe*, in the Solent. The Royal Yacht sliced the smaller vessel in half and despite the efforts of her crew several *Mistletoe* sailors and the sister-in-law of the owner were drowned. The Solent was crowded with shipping at the time and the *Alberta*, commanded by Prince Victor of Leiningen, the Queen's nephew, was said to be making 17 knots.

Disaster strikes! The *Alberta*, a favourite yacht of Queen Victoria, runs down and sinks the *Mistletoe* in the Solent, 18 August 1875. The Queen was on board at the time and there were several deaths on the *Mistletoe*.

At the Board of Inquiry convened by the Admiralty to look into the disaster, blame was laid at the door of Captain Welch, the Staff Captain on the *Alberta*, who was reprimanded for not having taken enough care and attention over his duties. Prince Victor was exonerated, the board concluding that his attention at the time was unavoidably taken up by 'attendance on the Queen.'

Many disagreed with the conclusion and when it later transpired that Victoria had sent a letter to the Prince, supporting him in his time of troubles, there was considerable bad feeling. Prince Victor was actually hissed and booed as he rode through the streets of Portsmouth. Victoria simply put it down to the 'rougher elements' of the town.

Despite the accident, Victoria continued to use the *Alberta*. And, in fact, it was this tiny ship that carried the Queen's body from the Isle of Wight to Portsmouth on 1 February 1901. The Queen had died at Osborne House on 22 January; two weeks later the *Alberta* took her on her final journey.

The vessel left the Isle of Wight in the afternoon and entered the Solent shortly after 3.00 p.m., just as the sun was beginning to sink below the horizon. The sky was, apparently, a wonderful golden pink with smoke from the guns of the attendant warships hanging in a long festoon across the sea. Cissy, Countess of Denbigh, wrote:

> Slowly, down the long line of battleships, came eight torpedo destroyers, dark gliding forms, and after them the white *Alberta* looking very small and frail next to the towering battleships ... As slowly and as silently as it came, the cortege passed away into the haze with the solemn booming of the guns continuing every minute till Portsmouth was reached.[18]

The *Alberta* outlived her mistress by a bare twelve years. Finally declared obsolete, she was broken up in 1913.

The *Enchantress*, launched on 2 August 1862, was never a Royal Yacht although many have labelled her as exactly that. She was, in fact, a yacht built for the Admiralty, a twin-screw vessel that was used for what was euphemistically called 'particular service'. In 1912, for example, she took Winston Churchill, then First Lord of the Admiralty, on a summer cruise and she did, sometimes provide service for the royal family.

The battleship *Renown*, launched at the dockyard in May 1895, was one of three light battleships built for colonial wars. However, she was seriously under-armed, with 10-inch guns that could not even begin to challenge the might of other European warships. Despite this drawback she was an elegant vessel. Jacky Fisher, later the First Sea Lord, first saw her on the American Station and fell in love with her broad teak decks and high speed. He took her with him when he assumed command in the Mediterranean. She was exactly the type of vessel he wanted for the 'social' events required of a peacetime navy.

It was an emotion that was reciprocated by members of the royal family and by those in the higher echelons of the navy. The *Renown* was commissioned to take the Duke and Duchess of Connaught on a tour to India in November 1902 and was so successful in this role that, although she returned to the Mediterranean Fleet in March 1903, she was clearly marked down for other duties.

The end of an era. The *Alberta* passes up the Solent in February 1901, carrying the body of Queen Victoria who had died on the Isle of Wight a few days earlier. Taken from an engraving by the marine artist W. L. Wylie.

The Admiralty Yacht *Enchantress*, launched in 1862 and used to take dignitaries like Winston Churchill on summer cruises.

The battleship *Renown*, favourite of Admiral Jacky Fisher, was used as a Royal yacht on long-distance tours. She is shown here in her Victorian paintwork and regalia.

On 21 February 1905 she was taken to Portsmouth for conversion into a Royal Yacht. Her secondary armament was removed and in October the same year she took the Prince and Princess of Wales for another tour around India. Following that she was attached to the Home Fleet as 'a subsidiary yacht.'

Between October and December 1907 the *Renown* carried King Alfonso XIII and Queen Victoria Eugenia of Spain on an official trip to Britain but, thereafter, was judged to be surplus to requirements. In 1909 she became a training ship for stokers and was sold for scrap in 1914.

The last Royal Yacht to be launched from Pembroke Dockyard was yet another *V and A*, the *Victoria and Albert* (III). She slid into the waters of Milford Haven on 9 May 1899, the first non-paddle Royal Yacht of Victoria's reign. She had been laid down after Victoria petitioned Parliament for a more modern and up to date Royal Yacht. Both the Kaiser of Germany and the Czar of Russia, she claimed, had newer vessels and national pride, at the very least, demanded Britain should be the owner of a better Royal Yacht than other European nations.

Designed by Sir William White, Chief Constructor of the Navy, the *Victoria and Albert* (III) was 380 feet in length, 40 foot in the beam and cost a total of £572,000 to build. Unfortunately, the ship was somewhat top heavy, the extra weight coming from several topside additions – including a large traditional capstan so that the Queen could be entertained by watching her sailors at work.

The result of this top heaviness was near disaster. Shortly after her launch the *Victoria and Albert* actually keeled over when the dry dock in which she had been accommodated was flooded in order to float her out. Thanks to quick thinking by dockyard staff there was minimal damage but there were, naturally enough, grave concerns about the stability of the ship and the safety of the Queen.

On 4 January 1900 the *Victoria and Albert* was taken out to a buoy in the river and 400 dockyard maties were ferried aboard. They were then made to run from one side of the ship to the other in order to check her stability. Luckily for the workmen she did not capsize but a Court of Inquiry was held and the top heaviness of the vessel was remarked on. Sir William White felt obliged to tender his resignation. He retired, a broken man.

And the Queen? She was supposedly unhappy about the ship but never actually got to see her or set foot upon her. The Royal Yacht was not completed and declared ready for service until late in 1901 and by then Victoria had been dead for seven months.

The *Victoria and Albert* (III) went on to make sixty voyages before 1914, when the outbreak of war ended such indulgences, and to serve four different monarchs – Edward VII, George V, Edward VIII and George VI. After the end of the First World War she was, in the main, confined to home waters. A sumptuous yacht, the height of luxury, she was never totally satisfactory as a sea boat, being too large and too unwieldy to carry out what was asked of her.

As a result of the Admiralty's unhappiness with the *V and A* she was supplemented by the Royal yacht *Alexandra*, built by the firm of A. & J. Inglis of Glasgow, a ship that was sunk by German dive bombers during the Norwegian Campaign of 1940, long after she had passed out of royal use.

The launch of the third and final *Victoria and Albert* at Pembroke Dock in May 1899. Queen Victoria died before she could use her but the large and ornate yacht served several other monarchs across the years.

The elegant lines of the *Victoria and Albert* can be clearly seen on this early postcard view.

The *Victoria and Albert* (III) remained in commission until 1939. During the Second World War she served as an accommodation and depot ship for the training school HMS *Excellent*. She was finally towed out of Portsmouth for the breakers yard on 1 December 1954.

As an interesting postscript, during the *V and A*'s construction in 1899 two gold sovereigns had been placed under the truck of one of her masts, as tradition demanded. When she was broken up in 1954 Pembroke Borough Council wrote to Queen Elizabeth asking for the coins to be returned. Not unnaturally, the request was refused.

The last *Victoria and Albert* was succeeded by the *Britannia*, the first Royal Yacht since the 1840s not to have been built at Pembroke Dock. But the *Britannia* did visit the Haven and Pembroke Dock in 1954, bringing the new Queen Elizabeth on a visit to the town. She was the first monarch to set foot in Pembroke Dock since Edward VII landed in the Dockyard in August 1902.

King Edward VII visits Pembroke Dock – something his mother had never done – coming ashore from the Royal Yacht *Victoria and Albert* and landing within the dockyard.

The king is taken on a tour of south Pembrokeshire before returning to the dockyard and sailing away – never to return.

7

Accident, Collision and the Odd Sinking

No ship, however well built, is infallible. At the end of the day a ship is only a tool and the decisions and actions of the men who sail her inevitably have a bearing on the vessel's success or failure. Sometimes a combination of bad design, poor workmanship, ill luck and rank bad handling come together – and when they do it invariably spells disaster.

Many Pembroke Dock ships had unfortunate accidents at various stages of their careers. Sometimes they were able to escape with just the odd scratch or two, sometimes the accidents resulted in complete disaster.

The *Janus* and *Drake*, two 238-ton gunboats launched at 5.30 in the afternoon of 8 March 1856, caused mayhem on the very day of their launch. They were to be launched from the same slipway and, consequently the launching platform was actually situated half way down the slip, between the two vessels.

The platform was crowded with dignitaries and officials as the *Janus* was named and began to move. Unfortunately, she caught the edge of the launching platform, totally demolishing it and pitching the guests to the ground. Mrs Mathias of Lamphey Court, who was performing the ceremony, and her two children, were tossed around like matchsticks. The children were shocked but otherwise unhurt. Mrs Mathias, however, was taken away to hospital where she was treated for a broken collar bone.

The cruiser *Thames*, launched in December 1885, also encountered difficulties before she began her career. Her engines were being tested alongside the fitting out berth at Hobbs Point when the yacht *May*, one of many small vessels crowding the waterway to look at the new ship, came too close and was dragged in by the suction of the cruiser's propellers.

Before anyone realised, the *May*'s stern was under water and her hull was smashed to pieces by the cruiser's giant propellers. The owner William Ribbon, Edwin Traylor and several other local dignitaries managed to jump clear and swim to safety. Despite the heroism of Captain Greenland, one of the passengers on the yacht, young William Bray was pulled under and drowned. His body was recovered from the river several days later.

The *Thames* saw no action as a cruiser but in 1903 she was converted into one of the navy's first submarine depot ships. She returned to Milford Haven a year later,

The ill-fated HMS *Montagu* aground on the rocks at Shutter Point, Lundy. Despite the best efforts of Pembroke Dockyard workmen, she could not be saved. (*J&C McCutcheon Collection*)

taking part in exercises in the Dale Roads along with early Holland Class submarines. In 1920 the *Thames* was bought by South African entrepreneur T. B. Davies and, in memory of his son, was presented to a Trust and run as a training ship. Renamed *General Botha* she was based at Simonstown, serving as an accommodation ship during the Second World War before being broken up in 1947.

The *Prince Consort* was the first iron-cased ship to be launched from Pembroke Dockyard on 26 June 1862. Originally called *Triumph*, at the last minute her name was changed in memory of the late Prince Consort. A large vessel of 4,045 tons, she was armed with eleven 7-inch and twenty-four 68-pdr guns. On passage to Liverpool to oversee Confederate 'rams' then being built for the rebel states of America, she ran into an Irish Sea gale. It was her first time at sea and no-one had any real idea of how she would handle. The answer was 'Badly'.

The *Prince Consort* began to take on water and it quickly transpired that there was a serious design flaw. She simply did not have enough scuppers to allow the water coming on board in such a heavy sea to drain away. As a result the new ship very nearly foundered on her first voyage. She survived, alterations were made and the ship duly took her place in the Channel and, then, the Mediterranean Fleets.

Interestingly, the *Prince Consort* was renowned as the second worst 'roller' in the navy, after another Pembroke Dock ship, the *Lord Clyde*. Possibly this was down to her construction. She had been designed and had actually begun life as a wooden line-of-battle warship but in June 1861 work began to refit her with armour plating. Never totally successful, she was eventually sold in 1882 and was duly broken up.

The *Prince Consort*, Pembroke Dockyard's first ironclad screw vessel, almost sank on her maiden voyage when she hit a gale in the Irish Sea – there were not enough scuppers to allow the water taken on board during the storm to run away.

The *Lord Clyde*, along with her Chatham-built sister ship *Lord Warden*, was the last of the true broadside ironclads. Thereafter the guns on all capital ships were mounted fore and aft. Famous throughout the Navy as the worst 'roller' afloat, on sea trials in 1867 she had even rolled her gunports below water and was clearly not usable as a fighting ship in anything like a heavy sea.

She came off the stocks at Pembroke Dock on 27 May 1865, a massive ship with the main skin of her hull consisting of 24-inch thick timber, bound by one and a half inches of iron. A 4-inch belt of oak ran around her hull at the waterline.

Serving with the Mediterranean Fleet, she was lying at Syracuse when in March 1872 a telegram was received from Fleet Headquarters in Malta. A British steamer had gone aground on the island of Pantellaria and the *Lord Clyde* was to proceed there and tow her off. Unfortunately, during the rescue operations the warship herself ran aground – her anchors were laid out, coal was jettisoned and the guns were even hoisted over the side into small boats. It was no use, she was stuck fast.

An officer was dispatched to Malta on a passing steamer with the news and the *Lord Warden* arrived to pull off her sister ship. It was a difficult task and the damage *Lord Clyde* had sustained was soon apparent to everyone. The tow to Malta took three days with the battleship leaking at a rate of two feet per hour. She was then taken back to Britain, a long and arduous exercise, but despite the best efforts of dockyard workers she never saw active service again.

Helping other vessels in trouble seems to have been a common but dangerous operation. The sloop *Harrier* spent the Crimean War in the Baltic but in October 1860

Large and unwieldy, one of the worst 'rollers' in the navy, the *Lord Clyde* was taken out of commission after running aground during rescue operations in the Mediterranean.

she was sent out to the Australian Station. She was involved in punitive actions against the natives of Fiji in 1863 but that same year she was detailed to take part in rescue operations on HMS *Orpheus*.

The *Orpheus* had been wrecked in Manukau Harbour and attempts were being made to pull her off the shallow reef where she lay. The *Harrier* quickly found herself grounded on the same shallow shoal, much to the indignation and embarrassment of the officers in charge. It took some time but the *Harrier* was eventually freed without too much damage. It was, in many respects, a lucky escape for the small vessel.

On 2 January 1879 a major gun explosion took place on the battleship *Thunderer*. The ship had been launched from Pembroke Dock on 26 March 1872, a revolutionary vessel, only the second mastless, sea-going turret ship in the navy. Together with her sister ship *Devastation* (built at Portsmouth, not Pembroke Dock) she was for a time the most powerful warship in the world. The *Devastation*, incidentally, is the one Victorian ship of which almost everyone has seen an image. She was the ship that featured on the front of Bryant & May matchboxes, production of which only finished in 1994.

The *Thunderer*'s four 12-inch guns were muzzle loaders and when on exercise in the Sea of Marmara in 1879 one of those guns failed to fire. By oversight, the gun crew did not realise what had happened and proceeded to reload. It meant that one of the barrels was now double loaded.

When the *Thunderer* fired again, the gun simply exploded. It wrecked the turret and killed eleven men. The tragedy was devastating and the Admiralty made the decision that, from that point on, they would use only breech loading guns in all new ships.

The *Thunderer* was not new to disaster. Shortly after her launch, in 1876, she was on exercise in Stokes Bay when an explosion in one of her box boilers rocked the ship. Forty-five sailors were killed including the captain, who just happened to be in the engine room at that moment. Seventy men were seriously injured in the explosion. The accident signalled the end of box boilers on RN ships, the disaster being caused by a broken pressure gauge and seized up safety valves.

The *Thunderer* went on to serve for many years, being modified and given triple expansion engines in 1881, something that doubled her range and halved fuel consumption. King George V served on board as a Lieutenant during his naval service and between May 1895 and December 1900 she operated as Guard Ship at Pembroke Dock – one of the few Pembroke Dock vessels to have any connection with the town and dockyard after her launch. She was finally sold for scrapping in July 1909.

One of the most tragic events ever to befall a Pembroke Dock vessel was the loss of the training ship *Atalanta*. Launched in July 1844 as the *Juno*, a sixth rate frigate of twenty-six guns, she took part in the annexing of the Cocos Islands in 1857 and served on the North American Station for many years before returning home in January 1878 and being re-christened *Mariner*.

The new name lasted just two weeks before she was re-named yet again, this time as the *Atalanta* – an original Pembroke Dock sloop of this name having been broken up in 1868. The new *Atalanta* was to operate as a sea-going training ship for the navy, giving young sailors a taste of life on board a fully rigged sailing ship.

On 31 January 1880 the *Atalanta* left Bermuda, with a crew of 113 sailors and 170 trainees, bound for Falmouth. She was never seen again. Somewhere in the Atlantic she ran into a powerful storm and with Captain Stirling's concerns about her propensity to roll being well recorded, it is fairly clear what happened. A major search

The battleship *Thunderer*, one of the most revolutionary vessels of the nineteenth century, was also an unlucky ship. A boiler explosion and an accident in one of her gun turrets caused many deaths on board.

operation was mounted but all that was ever discovered was a quantity of wreckage, broken spars and pieces of timber.

Public opinion was outraged, the Admiralty apparently receiving somewhere in the region of 200 letters from distraught relatives and friends of the trainees. *The Times* fulminated about the 'criminal folly' of sending out youngsters, many of whom had rarely been to sea before, in such conditions and the Admiralty promptly suspended all sea-going training for young boys. Among those lost was Philip Fisher, the younger brother of future First Sea Lord Jacky Fisher.

The loss of the *Atalanta* was a tragedy but other sinkings were neither as dramatic nor as fatal. The loss of the wooden despatch vessel *Psyche* on 15 December 1870 was one example. Launched from the dockyard in 1862 at a cost of £43,000, she was wrecked off Catania in Italy while carrying a party of scientists and geographers to observe a solar eclipse from Sicily.

Included in the party on board was the brother of Charles Darwin and several other notable men, all of whom were taken off before the ship sank. The wreck remained partially above water but was considered a danger to navigation. The remains of the *Psyche* were therefore blown up in February 1871.

When the *Iron Duke* (launched from the dockyard on St David's Day 1870) and the *Vanguard* collided in the Irish Sea on 1 September 1875 it was the meeting of two naval giants. The two ships were part of the Reserve Training Squadron and in company with *Warrior* and *Hector* sailed from Dun Laoghaire (then called Kingstown) en route for Cobh, outside Cork.

Just south of Dublin, they ran into dense fog and although sailing in line ahead there were no specific orders about what action to take in the event of such weather conditions. To make matters worse, the *Vanguard* had no working foghorn and was sailing directly ahead of the *Iron Duke*.

The Officer of the Watch ordered the *Iron Duke* to change course but, unfortunately, at almost the same moment the *Vanguard* did exactly the same in order to avoid a small sailing ship that had suddenly come into view. With a roar that could be heard on the Irish mainland, the two warships collided, the *Iron Duke*'s ram tearing a hole in the side of the *Vanguard*, close to the engine room.

Water immediately poured into the stricken ship, quenching her boilers and stopping the steam driven pumps. Within an hour she had sunk. All 360 members of the crew were got across to the *Iron Duke*, the only fatality being a pet dog which, apparently, jumped into the sea in panic.

At the Court of Inquiry, Captain Richard Dawkins of the *Vanguard* was blamed for the disaster and duly dismissed while the Officer of the Watch on board the *Iron Duke* was also dismissed from the ship. The navy initially tried to salvage the wreck but it was an impossible task and she was left to lie on the sandy seabed in around160 feet of water. She remains there to this day, lying on her starboard side and largely intact.

The ironclad *Anson*, launched in February 1886, also managed to inflict a mortal wound on another ship, this time the liner *Utopia*. On 17 March 1891 the *Utopia*, full of Italian emigrants on their way to a new life in the USA, swept into the Bay of Gibraltar. It was a dark, windy night and the *Anson* was lying peacefully in the

The *Iron Duke*, launched from the yards in 1870, had the misfortune to hit and sink her sister ship *Vanguard* in the Irish Sea.

The *Vanguard*, not Pembroke Dock built, but sunk by the *Iron Duke* in a fog while en route to Cork on 1 September 1875. All the crew got off safely, the only casualty being a pet dog which leapt overboard in panic.

The battleship *Anson* was involved in a collision with the liner *Utopia* at Gibraltar in March 1891. Hundreds of Italian emigrants, heading for a new life in the USA were drowned in the accident.

warship anchorage. By a terrible error of judgement, the *Utopia* found herself in the wrong part of the harbour and almost before her crew knew what was happening, scraped across the ram bow of the warship.

A huge hole nearly twenty feet wide was gouged out of the liner's side and she sank in twenty minutes, taking 562 of her passengers and crew with her to the bottom. Two would-be rescuers from the *Immortalite* – yet another Pembroke Dock ship – also died that night.

Captain John McKeague of the *Utopia* was blamed for the accident and the loss of life. He claimed to have been dazzled by the *Anson*'s searchlights and was considering beaching his ship but she suddenly developed a 20 degree list and turned over, crushing those lifeboats that had been launched. Whatever the rights and wrongs, only 218 people were saved from the sinking ship.

One shipwreck that involved Pembroke Dock workmen, although she was not actually a Pembroke Dock ship, was that of the *Montagu*, lost on Lundy in 1906. In a thick fog the Duncan-Class battleship drove onto the rocks of Shutter Point just after 2.00 a.m. on 30 May and despite all attempts to free her, found herself stuck fast.

Workmen from Pembroke Dockyard were taken out to Lundy, where they were accommodated in the Marisco Castle cottages. Here they endured harsh conditions – in the cottages, on the windswept island and on the decks of the ship itself. In the end, it proved impossible to save the *Montagu* and the wreck was slowly battered to pieces by the Bristol Channel gales. The dockyard workmen were more than happy to head home:

> The heavy and incessant work and lack of sleep had put a considerable strain on the nerves of the men – they had been working like Trojans, labouring continuously for as much as thirty hours at a stretch. These conditions had already led to some disorder aboard, and the final 'down tools' resulted in a few thirsty workers breaking into the island canteen and helping themselves … Several of the imbibers suffered injury through falling over the cliffs, and paid for their misdemeanors in broken limbs and bruises.[19]

Many more Pembroke Dock ships were lost or sunk by accident. These include the *Spey*, wrecked in the West Indies in 1840, and four more of her sister ships (Cherokee-Class sloops built in the yards in the 1820s and 1830s). They really were an unlucky group of ships, the *Skylark* being cast up on the rocks of the Isle of Wight and the *Thais* being lost with all hands while on passage to Halifax in 1833.

The *Imogene*, launched in June 1831 was accidentally burned at Plymouth in 1840 – fire was a dreaded fear for all wooden warships. Then there was the *Amazon*, one of the last timber-hulled sloops in the navy. She was commissioned in April 1866 and within a year she had collided with the steamer *Osprey* off Start Point. Both vessels sank but, fortunately, all hands were saved.

With some vessels, disaster came at the end of their working lives. The gunboat *Insolent* of 1881 was the second ship in her class and by the end of the First World War she was serving as the Gate Vessel on the boom at Portsmouth Dockyard. On 1 July 1922, for no apparent reason, she suddenly foundered and sank. The wreck was sold to the firm of J. H. Pounds of Portsmouth.

Not Pembroke Dock built but there was a Pembroke Dock connection with the battleship *Montagu* which struck Lundy Island in 1905.

Despite the efforts of dozens of Pembroke Dock workmen, the *Montagu* proved impossible to save. She was paid off and battered to death by the waves – the dockyard workmen went home, gratefully.

The gunboat *Gnat* was christened by Miss Mirehouse of Angle – in the dark! Perhaps the night time launch was an omen as within a year the *Gnat* had been ignominiously wrecked on an island in the China Sea.

There were so many other incidents involving Pembroke Dock ships, some fatal, others that merited little more than a simple entry in the ship's log, that it would take a whole book to do them full justice. Suffice to say that shipwreck, accident and sudden destruction were, quite literally, occupational hazards for all Victorian and Edwardian seamen.

8

Iron and Steel Take Over

In 1860 the iron clad *Warrior* was launched from the private dockyard of C. J. Mare. It was a pivotal moment in naval history as from the minute the *Warrior* slipped down the launching ways into the River Thames, every other ship in the world was rendered suddenly obsolete. She was the first iron clad ship in the world – although the French battleship *Gloire* had actually been laid down several months before – and her arrival spelled the end of wooden warships.

It also meant the end for dockyards like Pembroke Dock, unless they could adapt very quickly to the new techniques and skills now required for ship building. It was a challenge that Pembroke Dockyard was willing to face.

The *Howe*, a 120-gun ship of the line, and the 50-gun *Aurora*, launched in 1860 and 1861, were the last of their kind to leave the slipways at Pembroke Dock. The *Howe* was also the navy's last three-decker, a massive warship of 6,577 tons, twice the size of Nelson's *Victory*.

Adapting to new building techniques presented a major problem. The workmen at Pembroke Dock had been trained to build wooden ships. Working in metal was a different matter. Nobody doubted that the men would be able to adapt, to transfer their skills, but it would take time. And then, of course, there was the matter of the wooden ships currently in the process of being built.

Re-designing the part-built wooden ships was the first problem to be solved. Protective belts of armour were hastily installed into their hulls in an effort to give them at least a degree of protection from enemy ironclads. The *Prince Consort* of June 1862 was the first Pembroke Dock vessel to be altered in this way and she is therefore regarded as the dockyard's first iron clad warship.

In the wake of the *Warrior's* launch, the Admiralty set up a Royal Commission to examine the viability of the Royal Dockyards – the *Warrior* had, after all, been launched from a private yard. The first question the Commission had to answer was a simple one – were the Royal naval Dockyards really necessary? For a while the closure of the yards at Deptford, Woolwich, Sheerness and Pembroke Dock was given serious consideration. All of them were situated in the most inconvenient parts of the country but, in the end, only Deptford and Woolwich went under the axe.

In 1860 the *Warrior*, the first iron-built, armoured battleship the world had seen, was launched from the private yards of C. J. Mare on the Thames and overnight made every other ship in the world suddenly obsolete.

What saved Pembroke Dock was, first, the building of a railway link to the town and yards and, secondly – and perhaps more importantly – the advent of the composite warship.

Composite ships were, effectively, a compromise between the old style of ship building and the new. They consisted of iron frames over which was laid wooden planking. It was the ideal medium for the gunboats, sloops and other small craft so necessary to the Victorian navy and, of course, as far as Pembroke Dockyard was concerned the process could be guaranteed to use up the large stock of timber stored in the yards while exploiting the local shipwrights' undoubted skill in using it.[20]

Orders for Pembroke Dockyard to build two wooden sloops, the *Success* and *Sabrina*, were immediately cancelled and the yards began to produce a whole range of composite ships. Over the next dozen or so years the Admiralty also sold off huge quantities of teak and other wood from the dockyard, all surplus to requirements. Much of the wood was bought and used in the construction of doors, window frames and beams in the houses of the town.

The yards continued to build the occasional wooden ship, as long as the order and the demand were there. The last wooden vessel constructed in the yards came quite late in the history of the place and was the training brig *Mayflower*, launched on 20 January 1890.

The *Research*, launched on 15 August 1863, was an iron-cased sloop of 1,253 tons. She was originally intended as a wooden hulled vessel and was converted on the

The *Research*, launched from the yards in 1863, was converted from a wooden sloop. She was intended to be an experimental vessel, for trying out new armour and armaments, but was never totally successful.

building slip to designs drawn up by Sir Edward Reed. This was an age of experiment and the *Research*, it was quickly decided, would be exactly that – an experimental vessel in which new concepts, new ideas, could be tried out and developed.

As might be expected, she was never really successful and had grave drawbacks as a warship, somebody once branding her as the worst ship, both as a weapon of war and as a sea boat, ever to come out of a Royal Dockyard. To begin with she rolled excessively, a problem which often forced her to remain in harbour during winter months. Part of the problem with her stability undoubtedly came from the conversion from wood to iron, when her sloop bow and stern had been changed in order to give her a ram bow and rounded stern.

Slow in speed and always liable to ship water, the *Research* served with the Channel Fleet and in the Mediterranean but after only fifteen years in commission she was laid up in 1878 and scrapped six years later.

The *Gnat* was Pembroke Dockyard's first composite gunboat. Launched on 26 November 1867 she was followed, a year later, by the frigate *Inconstant*, also a composite warship. The *Gnat's* life was short, wrecked and sunk a year after her launch, but the *Inconstant* survived for many years. She was, in effect, Britain's first iron-hulled cruiser, being armed with ten 9-inch and six 7-inch rifled muzzle loaders, giving her the ability to fight at long range where her unarmoured hull would be less vulnerable.

Although unarmoured, the *Inconstant's* hull was subdivided, up to the main deck, by ten water-tight bulkheads and despite being extremely fast, achieving 16.5 knots, in shallow water, during her steaming trials, she and the rest of her class proved far too expensive to build. As a consequence the design was not repeated.[21]

The *Inconstant* of 1868 was the first of three steam assisted, fully-masted frigates with iron hulls.

The importance of the *Gnat* lies simply in the fact that she began a whole range of composite ships at Pembroke Dock. It was a building programme that lasted for over twenty years until 1889, when the sloop *Dlondo* became the last composite ship to be launched from Pembroke Dock.

The *Zealous* was launched on 7 March 1864. An ironclad frigate of 3,167 tons, she carried an armament of twenty 7-inch guns and became the first armoured ship to cross the Equator. In 1866 she also became the first armoured vessel to enter the Pacific Ocean. Sold out of the navy in the autumn of 1886, she was broken up at Charlton.

Progress in developing the skills necessary to build iron ships was both slow and uneven. The *Ajax* of 1882, for example, was a heavily armoured citadel ship armed with four 12-inch guns, two each end of her central castle.

Along with her sister ship *Agamemnon* (not built at Pembroke Dock) she was renowned as a poor sea boat, difficult to handle and very unwieldy. Barely able to make 13 knots, her bow and stern were unarmoured. The rationale behind this design was simple – if these had become waterlogged she would have foundered and the unarmoured ends were required to maintain buoyancy.

Progress in ship design was a constantly changing feast in the nineteenth century and just as wood had been replaced as the primary building material by iron, so steel eventually began to assume greater significance in warship design.

The dispatch vessels or cruisers *Iris* and *Mercury*, launched in 1877 and 1878, were not only the first steel vessels built at Pembroke Dock, they were actually the first steel vessels in the Royal Navy. From the beginning they were hugely effective and efficient ships.

On her sea trials the *Mercury* recorded a speed of 18 knots, making her the fastest warship afloat at that time. The *Iris* was not far behind with a speed of 17.5 knots. Originally equipped with light barque rig, the sails of both ships were soon removed, so making them the Navy's first 'mastless cruisers.'

The *Iris* finished her days as a tender to the training ship *St Vincent* in Portsmouth Harbour. The *Mercury*, slightly longer than her sister ship and with a somewhat different appearance, was so well thought of that she was re-armed three times during her life as a cruiser. She, also, spent some time as a training ship, becoming a navigation school for officers in 1903. She was then, in 1906, converted into a submarine depot ship before being hulked, taken to Rosyth under the new name of *Columbine* and broken up in 1919.

The most remarkable thing about the battleship *Edinburgh* was her very shallow draught. Launched on 18 March 1882, she was designed with the express purpose of transiting the Suez Canal and was named by the Duchess of Connaught. It was a day of celebrations in the yard as somewhere in the region of 20,000 came to witness the event.

The Duke and Duchess of Connaught, together with the Duke of Edinburgh, came ashore from their yacht at 1.00 p.m., greeted by a twenty-one gun salute from the Defensible Barracks on the hill above the town. The Castlemartin Yeomanry then escorted the party to the town's market hall, where they were met by the Mayor and the Corporation. The Dockyard gates were thrown open to the public just before 3.00 p.m. and the Regimental Band of the Duke of Cornwall's Light Infantry entertained the huge crowds with selections from Wagner, Strauss and Weber. While all this was going on the Chief Constructor explained the construction and idea behind the ship to the Duchess.

Finally, the Royal party ascended the launching platform. The Duchess pressed a button – embedded deeply in an array of flowers – and this caused the traditional bottle to break against the ship's side. There was a slight pause and then, amid deafening roars and cheers, the *Edinburgh* began to move. To the tune of 'Rule Britannia' and 'A Life on the Ocean Wave' the ship slipped into the river while 500 invited guests accompanied the launching party to an evening reception and dinner in the Dockyard.

Sadly, the *Edinburgh* was not a success. Her shallow draught meant that she constantly rolled in even the most moderate of seas. Despite this she survived until 1910, when she was finally sold to Ward's of Briton Ferry and broken up.

The *Iris*, shown here in her later role as a training ship. Along with her sister ship *Mercury*, she was the first steel hulled warship in the navy.

The launch of the battleship *Edinburgh* in 1882. In this contemporary print the Chief Constructor explains the vessel to the Royal party there for the launch. Note the shallow draught of the ship, designed to navigate the Suez Canal.

The *Doris*, a wooden screw frigate launched from the yards on 25 March 1857.

Left: Hoisting a ship's funnel onto a newly launched vessel. This shows the giant sheerlegs, essential lifting gear that all dockyards used in the days before cranes, in full operation.

Below: HMS *Dreadnought*, launched from Pembroke Dockyard in 1875 – who would have believed that a vessel of the same name would later spell the end of the road for the Welsh yards?

9

The Crimean War

When the Crimean War broke out in October 1853 it was the first time Britain had been involved in a major conflict since the Waterloo campaign of 1815. The war, a bungled and botched series of battles and campaigns, was fought between Russia on one side and an alliance of Britain, France and Turkey on the other. Put simply, it was part of a long-standing power contest between European nations to decide who would wield influence over the declining Ottoman Empire.

Most of the campaigning took place on the Crimean Peninsula but there were also actions in the Baltic, the Caucasus, the Pacific and in Anatolia. And while the war on the land was a mix of chaos and inefficiency, the sea campaigns – in which many Pembroke Dock ships took part – were far more effectively managed.

Sir Charles Napier commanded the Baltic Fleet, flying his flag in the *Duke of Wellington*. Included in his fleet was the *James Watt*, one of the last wooden two-deckers ever built for the Royal Navy. Launched from Pembroke Dock on St George's Day 1853 as the only ship ever to carry the name, she was virtually brand new but Napier was not happy with her performance.

In particular, her machinery, taken from the iron frigate *Vulcan*, was not strong enough to power such a large vessel which weighed in at 4,950 tons. In 1856 she was sent back home but despite the enormous sum of £5,706 being spent on alterations and modifications, it made only minor improvements in the performance of the ship. Not surprisingly, *James Watt* was broken up in 1875.

The Baltic Campaign quickly reached something of a deadlock. The Russian ships were badly outnumbered and so, wherever possible, their admirals confined the movement of their vessels to the areas around the forts that lined the Finnish and Russian coasts.

It quickly became clear that these Russian forts were well supplied and well constructed. Napier took one look and decided that fortresses like Sveaborg were far too heavily defended to warrant an outright assault. When he was eventually pressurized into attacking the fort and dockyards he deployed over 1,000 guns against the fortress – to absolutely no avail.

As a result, the fleet turned its attentions to other, less well defended parts of the coast. The paddle sloop *Dragon*, launched from the dockyard in1845, was part of

The *Duke of Wellington*, flagship of Admiral Napier in the Baltic.

Napier's fleet but, in the main, operated independently. On 15 April 1854 she captured the Russian brig *Patrioten*, much to the glee of the British crew as the capture meant a considerable amount of prize money once they returned home.

The *Dragon* took another prize, and earned more prize money, the following day when she captured the merchantman *Victor*. A few days later, along with the *Magicienne* and *Imperieuse*, she took yet another brig, the *Antoine* – rich pickings indeed for the crew of the Pembroke Dock ship.

On 22 May 1854 the *Dragon* was ordered to try her guns against Fort Gustafvard. It was an uneven contest, the *Dragon* boasting just a handful of weapons against the thirty-one cannon mounted in the fort. Damaged and in difficulties, the *Dragon* retired from the fray but had been repaired sufficiently to take part in the bombardment of Sveaborg the following year.

On 29 May 1855 the sloop *Swallow*, launched from Pembroke Dockyard only the year before, was part of an operation to seize the Straits of Kertsch and thereby dominate the Sea of Azov.

Lieutenant Burgoyne from the *Swallow*, along with two sailors from other ships in the fleet, landed near the town of Gerritchi where, despite heavy fire from the Russians, they set fire to a field of corn and destroyed valuable stores and equipment. A second similar operation on 3 June saw Burgoyne awarded the Victoria Cross, the recently introduced medal for gallantry under fire.

At the beginning of 1856 Admiral Napier was in the process of gathering together as many ships as he could find, prior to a sustained attack on Sveaborg. Fortunately – or unfortunately, depending on how you look at it – the war ended in February, before the assault could be made.

In the Black Sea, around the Crimean Peninsula, the war at sea proved to be a much tougher contest. Almost as soon as the siege of Sevastopol began in 1854 the Russians scuttled ships to protect the harbour and then took their cannons to use as land artillery. By the end of the year huge vessels such as the *Grand Duke Constantine*, the *City of Paris* and the *Empress Maria* had all gone to the bottom.

In February 1855 they sank a second group of ships, in a line across the creek which joined Sevastapol Harbour to the Black Sea. And in September they burned all of the remaining vessels in their Black Sea Fleet. In effect the Royal Navy had wiped out the Russian's maritime might in the east without ever having to go into a Fleet action.

However, the four-mile creek into Sevastopol harbour was guarded by two huge forts, Constantine on the north, Alexander on the south, and attempts to destroy these – and other smaller forts along the waterway – occupied much of the navy's time.

The Pembroke Dock built *Rodney* and *Vengeance* both took part in a bombardment of the forts in October 1854 when their 90- and 84 gun broadsides were hugely effective, even though at one stage the *Rodney* went aground, her rigging on fire. She was towed off with her last intact hawser!

Interestingly, both the battleships were sailing craft, two of the earliest Pembroke Dock big gun ships, and had to be towed into position by steam driven vessels. The *Rodney* was pulled into action by the paddler *Spiteful*, launched from Pembroke Duckyard in 1842.

The Pembroke Dock-built sloop *Dragon* is shown here on 22 May 1854, bombarding Gustafvard Fort during the Baltic Campaign of the Crimean War.

HMS *Rodney* attacks Fort Constantine during the battle and bombardment of Sevastopol in 1854.

The *Vengeance*, twentieth warship launched from Pembroke Dock on 27 July 1824, is shown here in action in the Black Sea during the Crimean War.

The *Rodney* and *Vengeance* were the only two sailing ships not to be sent home for the winter of 1854. It was a hard and cruel couple of months, the weather bitterly cold and snow constantly falling. On 14 November a severe gale hit the area and twenty-one ships, most of them store vessels, were lost. The *Rodney* shipped a particularly heavy sea over her bows, the water sweeping her upper deck and flooding the captain's cabin.

The *Rodney* and *Vengeance* were then moored stem to stern in a creek, where they acted as rest centres for the troops. It is hardly the accustomed view of the campaign which, traditionally, portrays those in charge dismally failing to care for their men. On the contrary, compassion, it seems, was not an alien concept to all of the army commanders.

The paddle sloop *Inflexible*, launched in April 1845, was already in the Eastern Mediterranean when war broke out. And straight away she found herself being continuously worked. On 14 September 1853 she was sent to Rhodes carrying a surgeon who was to help deal with a smallpox outbreak on the island. In February the following year she was escorting Turkish transports across the Black Sea.

From March 1854 until April 1855 she was based at Varne, from where she made regular trips to Constantinople for supplies or to the main fleet at Sevastapol with despatches. On 6 June, along with the *Firebrand*, she captured six enemy merchant vessels carrying much needed supplies to the Russians. Then, on 17 July, she was part of a small force attacking the coastal town of Sulina. The attack left the town ablaze.

As if all this was not enough, in October 1855, in company with French warships, the *Inflexible* attacked enemy troops seen to be moving along the shore near Fort Nikolaev near the mouth of the River Dneiper. In March the following year she rescued sixty men when three British transports were wrecked on the Black Sea coast.

After all that the *Inflexible* and her crew had earned a well-deserved rest and the ship returned to Britain via Smyrna, Malta and Tripoli. She was sold out of the navy in 1864.

The Crimean War was notable for the use of Naval Brigades. Of course sailors had been used in land campaigns before but it was during this new conflict that Naval Brigades came into their own. And more importantly, they provided a much-needed fillip to the soldiers:

> The disasters of the Crimean War have lost none of their power to shock. Among those whose heroism brightened the gloom were a small force of sailors and marines, known as the 'Naval Brigade,' landed to help the British Army in its hour of need.[22]

A Naval Brigade could be a large number of sailors or very few. There was no set pattern or formula but members of the Brigades were extremely professional, both in their soldiering and in the very necessary business of foraging – at which they quickly outstripped all of the soldiers they encountered. Serving ashore quickly became accepted as normal for sailors. The navy did not fight one single major ship to ship action in the late Victorian period and those sailors who did see action did so as part of a Naval Brigade.[23]

Above: Sailors of the British Naval brigade, many of whom came from the Pembroke Dock-built *Rodney* and *Vengeance*, are shown here manning the guns during the siege of Sevastopol.

Left: A Harry Payne postcard showing an incident during the Crimean War, one of the worst managed wars in British history.

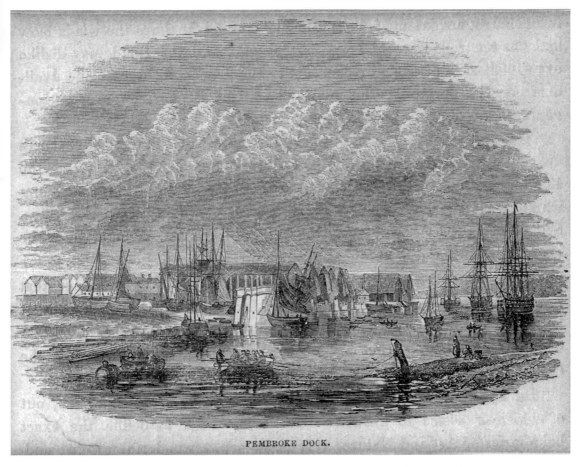

PEMBROKE DOCK.

A print from 1861 showing the building sheds at Pembroke Dock – just churning out vessels for the Royal Navy.

Pembroke Dock ships provided many sailors for such duties during the Crimean War and two men from the *Rodney* won Victoria Crosses while serving ashore with the Naval Brigade. Bosun's Mate John Sullivan won his medal for taking forward a flagstaff to act as an aiming point for the guns while under severe enemy fire. Bosun's Mate Henry Curtis ran over seventy yards of open ground to help a wounded man, carrying him back to safety through a hail of gunfire.

In the years to come, in campaigns right across the globe, the use of Naval Brigades became commonplace. They were central to Britain's naval power and prestige – in a navy that had no real competitor at sea, the use of sailors ashore ably demonstrated the power of the Empire and the professional nature of its most potent force, the Royal Navy.

10

Exploration

The nineteenth century was the great age of discovery. Scientific and statistical societies flourished and there was an enormous desire to push at the boundaries of knowledge. Exploration of the 'Dark Continent', as Africa was called, of the Arctic and Antarctic, of Australia and Far East were at the forefront of everyone's mind. As might be expected, Pembroke Dock ships played their part.

Named after the mythological dark region of Hades, the *Erebus* was a Hecla Class Bomb Vessel launched on 7 June 1826. She served for two years in the Mediterranean before being refitted as an exploration ship for the Arctic and Antarctic regions. On 21 November 1840, under the command of Captain James Clark, she left Tasmania for Antarctica, her first trip to what was then known as 'the great ice barrier'.

By January 1841 members of her crew had landed on Victoria Land and Mount Erebus on Ross Island – at 12,447 ft, the second highest volcano in Antarctica – was named after the ship. The *Erebus* soon returned to Tasmania but was back in the ice fields the following year, this time in company with the *Terror*, collecting oceanographic data and observing bird life. It was supposed to become a regular pattern as, at the end of the 1842 'exploring season', the ships sailed to the Falkland Islands, where they were due to be refitted. However, the *Erebus* was brought back to Britain, where she was fitted with steam engines, a converted version of those used in railway trains.

The next voyage of the *Erebus*, again in company with the *Terror*, was under Sir John Franklin. The ships left Greenhithe for the Arctic on 26 May 1843, the aim of the voyage being to collect scientific data and to attempt a crossing of the Northwest Passage. They were last seen entering Baffin Bay in August 1845 and thereafter they simply disappeared.

A massive search was instigated but it was 1853 before the full facts became known. The *Erebus* and *Terror* had become ice bound and were abandoned by their crews. All 130 men died trying to trek overland, reports by local Inuits stating that some of the dying men resorted to cannibalism. When the remains of the crew were found, in the twentieth century, cut marks on the frozen bodies supported this theory. The *Erebus* and *Terror*, which carried enough provisions to last two or three years, have never

The *Erebus*, launched in June 1826. Originally a bomb ship, the strength of her hull made her ideal for conversion into a vessel for Arctic and Antarctic exploration. Along with the *Terror*, she was lost during Sir John Franklin's expedition to find a Northwest Passage in 1845.

been found and were presumably crushed by the ice – hence the decision by Franklin to abandon an otherwise secure base.

The *Alert* was a 750 ton sloop, launched in 1856 with a specially strengthened hull for Polar service. On 29 May 1875, in company with the *Discovery* and *Valorous*, she began a stormy crossing of the Atlantic before heading north. At Godhaven the *Valorous* left the small convoy; *Discovery* wintered in a bay on Grant Land, leaving only the *Alert* to plough relentlessly on.

On 31 August she passed into latitude 82 degrees north, higher than any ship had ever gone before. A month later a foot party from the ship, led by Commander A. H. Markham, broke the record for the highest point ever reached by man. Battling against soft, wet snow and weak ice, seven of the twenty-four-strong party were badly frostbitten, three of them subsequently having limbs amputated. Conditions were so bad, with the wind constant from the north, that the only way to keep baggage and clothing from freezing was to sleep on them.

With the winter now firmly upon them, men from the *Alert* were forced to entertain themselves during the long, freezing Arctic nights on board the ship. Every Thursday evening they held what were called 'Pops', a series of concerts, theatrical performances and readings when the following song was always popular:

The *Alert*, launched in May 1856, was converted for polar exploration and sailed for Antarctica in May 1875.

'The Grand Palaeocrystic Sledging Song'

Not very long ago
On the six foot floe
Of the palaeocrystic sea,
Two ships did ride
Mid the crashing of the tide –
The Alert and the Discovery.

One night in March 1876 the *Alert* recorded a temperature of minus 73.7, 105 degrees of frost. At one time there were thirty-six recorded cases of scurvy on board the ship and, finally, she was forced to head back to Britain. It had been a remarkable achievement, opening the way to further expeditions in the years ahead. The *Alert* ended her days as a lighthouse tender for the Canadian Marine Service.

The *Newport* was a 4-gun sloop, launched on 20 July 1867. In 1881, being considered surplus to requirements, she was sold into private hands and re-named *Pandora II* before being sold on again a few years later. This time her new owners were Russian and she was re-christened *Blencathra*. Under her third name, she took part in a Russian expedition to that country's remote and unexplored northern coast. Commanded by Joseph Wiggins, she also carried rails for the Trans-Siberian Railway up the Yenisey River.

The *Newport* had several names during her exploration career. She was re-christened the *Svyataya Anna* and *Blencathra* before being crushed by Arctic ice in 1912.

In 1912 the *Newport* was sold on yet again, this time to Georgy Brusilov, and re-named *Svyataya Anna*. She undertook her final expedition to the Arctic in 1912, with Brusilov in command. Tragically, she became trapped in the ice and her hull crushed. There were just two survivors and the remains of the old *Newport* have never been found.

Another Pembroke Dock vessel with exploration and surveying connections was the Philomel Class gunboat *Pandora*, launched on 7 February 1861. She was bought from the navy by Sir Allen Young and used by him for his Arctic voyages of 1875–76. Then he, too, sold her on, this time to the extrovert newspaper owner and Arctic enthusiast Gordon Bennett.

Bennett immediately re-christened the ship *Jeanette* and fitted her out for an expedition to attempt to reach the North Pole through the Bering Strait. The ship's hull was massively reinforced to stand the pressure of the Arctic ice pack and although now privately owned she sailed under the orders and the jurisdiction of the US Navy. She left San Francisco on 8 July 1879 and by August was in St Lawrence Bay in Siberia. From there she headed north.

It was the same sad story. The *Pandora/Jeanette* was caught and trapped in the ice near Wrangel Island and for over twelve months drifted northwards towards the Pole. Lieutenant Commander George De Long, commanding the ship, discovered a number of small islands – Jeanette, Henrietta and Bennett – and these were duly claimed for the USA.

The *Pandora* was launched at Pembroke Dock in February 1861 but was sold to private ownership in 1875. Resold to newspaper magnate Gordon Bennett in 1876 she was quickly fitted out for Arctic exploration, one of Bennett's many passions.

Re-named *Jeanette*, the *Pandora* sailed for the Arctic under American colours – this view shows her flying the Star Spangled Banner – and was lost there, crushed by the ice flows, in June 1881.

The sloop/gunboat *Fly*, launched in 1831, is shown here exploring off the coast of Australia.

Then, on the night of 12 June 1881, the pressure of the ice finally began to crush the ship's hull. De Long and the crew swiftly unloaded provisions onto the flow and by the following morning the ship had disappeared under the ice. What followed was a heroic struggle for survival. The men trekked off towards Siberia, hauling their long boats behind them. They eventually found open water but one boat capsized in a storm and eight men drowned.

The remaining two boats now became separated. De Long and his men died, one after the other. Only two members of the boat crew survived. The other boat was luckier, the Chief Engineer and eleven of his men reaching safety after an epic struggle of courage and endurance.

Exploration was not limited just to the frozen wastes and Pembroke Dock ships served all over the world, mapping and recording new lands and geographical features. The *Fly*, an 18-gun sloop designed by Professor Inman from the School of Naval Architecture and launched from Pembroke Dockyard on 25 August 1831, began life on the North American and West Indies Station.

Then, in December 1841, along with the cutter *Bramble*, she was commissioned to survey the Torres Strait and in the mid-1840s she charted many routes around Australia's north-east coast.

The *Fly* was particularly active around Whitsunday Island and the Capricorn Islands but she also surveyed the Gulf of Papua New Guinea, where the Fly River is named after the ship. She moved on to surveying work in the Pacific, including a four year voyage around the coast of New Zealand. Finally laid up as a coal hulk back in Devonport, she was broken up in 1903.

The *Meteor* was launched from the yards on 25 June 1823 as a 14-gun bomb ship. Like most bomb ships she was a sturdy little vessel despite her wooden construction, ideal for exploration and survey work. Renamed *Beacon* in 1832, she was converted into a survey vessel and between 1836 and 1842, under the command of Thomas Graves, she was involved in surveying various parts of the Mediterranean and its coast.

Earlier in her career, in September 1828, the *Meteor* had sailed along with two other vessels to demand the return of two British merchantmen captured by Barbary pirates. A blockade of Tangiers had to be instigated by the three ships before the British merchant vessels were released – surveying, dealing with pirates, all part of the service life of Pembroke Dock ships.

A 28-gun sixth rate, launched in August 1825, the *Success* sailed for Australia in late 1826, arriving at the mouth of the Swan River in March the following year. On board were numerous botanists and scientists, including Charles Fraser, the colonial botanist of New South Wales, who later wrote a book on the suitability of the area for settlement.

On 3 December 1829 the *Success* grounded on Carnac Reef, heeling over onto her side. The ship had to be stripped of fixtures, fittings and cargo before she could be re-floated. In 1832 she returned to Britain but not before Success Bank, the town of Success and several other parts of Western Australia had been named after her.

The *Nassau* of 1866 was originally designated as a gun vessel or sloop but was converted to a survey ship before her launch. Between 1866 and 1880 she carried out

The sloop *Success*, one of the early ships launched from the yards in 1825, is shown here grounded on Carnac Reef in 1829 when surveying the Australian coast.

extensive surveys of the Magellan Straits before heading for home and the breakers yard.

The *Starling*, a small cutter with a crew of just thirty, led an active service life with battle honours that included the Opium Wars with China. Three of her crew died during those wars when she was commanded by Henry Kellett. She is best remembered, however, for her survey work in the waters around Hong Kong where Starling Inlet was named after her.

Canada was the scene for much of the *Egeria*'s career. Launched in 1873 and named after a Greek water nymph, she was involved in the Russo-Turkish War of 1877 when she was sent on what was termed an 'intelligence gathering mission' to Petropavlovsk and quickly ascertained that the Russians had abandoned the port.

Egeria then served on the Australian Station, carrying out a series of surveys under the command of Captain Pelham Aldrich before, in 1898, being sent to survey the waters around British Columbia. She remained in the area until 1911 when she was sold to the Vancouver Branch of the Navy League.

Her new role did not last long and in 1914 she was sold for breaking. Beached at Burrard Inlet, her hull was soaked in oil and the old ship was set ablaze. The *Egeria* did not go quietly, however. A huge explosion suddenly rocked the cove, the flames having reached a combustible part of the ship. Three workmen were killed by the explosion.

11

Gunboat Diplomacy

In the Victorian Age, when the answer to most colonial problems or difficulties seemed to be 'Send a gunboat', it was inevitable that Pembroke Dock ships were heavily involved in the skirmishes and small campaigns of the day.

The name gunboat is something of a generic term for the vessels that succeeded the earlier wooden sloops and cutters. Dispatch vessels and third- or even second- class cruisers were, really, no more than gunboats. They were small, shallow draught vessels, usually lightly armed but capable of responding quickly to problems of insurrection or revolt in Britain's colonies.

Several Pembroke Dock ships were involved in the Opium Wars against China – an amazing series of wars fought between 1838 and 1860 to allow the British the right to import opium into the country. They took place before the true evils of drug abuse were known but, even so, the thought of fighting a war in support of the opium trade (which, in turn, funded the growing habit of tea drinking across the Empire) seems nothing short of bizarre.

The *Imogene*, launched in 1831, had already seen service around the Indian coast and off Australia when she was sent to China in 1834. She was soon in action against the Chinese forts at the mouth of the Pearl River, in company with another Pembroke Dock ship, the *Andromache*. For two days there was intermittent action before the forts were silenced – at a cost of two killed and seven wounded on board the *Imogene*.

During the second of these Opium Wars, the Chinese were apparently so frightened of the power and size of the *Barracouta*, launched from Pembroke Dockard in March 1851 as the last paddle sloop ever to be built for the navy, that they offered £50,000 for her destruction.[24] The reward was unclaimed and the *Barracouta* went on to serve in the Anglo-Ashanti Wars and on the Australian Station, where she was involved in operations against the Samoans. After some time as a tender in Portsmouth Dockyard she was finally broken up at Chatham in 1881.

The *Gorgon* of 1837 was part of Charles Napier's squadron during the Syrian War, the climax of which came in the bombardment and capture of St Jean d'Acre on 3 November 1840. British salvos hit the magazine of the fortress, causing it to explode in a spectacular eruption. As Lieutenant Kerr on board the *Gorgon* later recalled, it was:

... the most awfully grand sight I ever saw, equal for the time, I should say, to any eruption of Vesuvius. Immense stones came tumbling down upward of a minute after it occurred, and an immense cloud of earth and dust, about four or five hundred feet high, moved slowly with the breeze, completely hiding the ships as it passed them.[25]

Approximately twenty ships took part in the bombardment, steam frigates like the *Gorgon* being used to tow line-of-battle ships into action. The frigates had to take care as they came under fire from the shore and if their vulnerable paddle wheels had been hit they would have been helpless in the water.

The *Bittern*, launched in December 1869 and the *Coquette* of 1871 were just two of many Pembroke Dock ships involved in the Anglo-Egyptian War of 1882. The war began with a coup by Colonel Ahmed Orabi but, unfortunately for him, Britain and France supported the deposed Khedive. Security of the Suez Canal was probably behind the British stance although there are those who deny that the Canal was ever in jeopardy and that British involvement was more of a political move on the part of Prime Minister William Gladstone and the Liberal Party.

Whatever the motives, British and French ships arrived off Alexandria on 20 May 1882 and a three day bombardment began on 11 July. The gunboat *Bittern*, armed with just a single 7-inch muzzle loader and two 40-pdrs, could not have added much to the bombardment but she played her part, operating close inshore and being, therefore, open to return fire from the Egyptian land batteries.

Similarly, the *Coquette*, a tiny vessel of just four guns, moved close inshore and contributed her part to the awesome array of shells that were raining down onto the Egyptian city. She later took part in the occupation of Ismalia, her crew serving as part of the Naval Brigade, and also fought at the Battle of Tofrik.

Several of the Victorian 'Little Wars' yielded gallantry medals for sailors serving on Pembroke Dock ships. Notable among these was the Victoria Cross given to Samuel

Opposite page: The sloop *Blanche*, one of many beautiful and sleek little vessels produced by Pembroke Dockyard in the nineteenth century.

Above: The bombardment of Alexandria during the Anglo-Egyptian war of 1882 – several Pembroke Dock ships were involved in the action.

Right: Operating an early form of Gatling Gun, sailors from the Naval Brigade help the army disperse insurgents during the Anglo-Egyptian War of 1882.

Mitchell, captain of the foretop on HMS *Harrier* during the Maori Wars in New Zealand. On 29 April 1864 in an action at Te Pape, a storming party of 150 members of the Naval Brigade from the *Harrier* and soldiers from the 43rd Light Infantry established a fortified position inside the town, known as Gate Pa.

During the charge towards the Gate, Commander Hay of the *Harrier* was mortally wounded but Mitchell brought him back to British lines, even though Hay ordered him not to expose himself to heavy and regular enemy fire. Samuel Mitchell was discharged from the navy in May 1865 and settled in New Zealand. He married and settled down to a life of farming. Unfortunately, things did not always run smoothly for Mitchell, despite fathering eleven children. Firstly, he lost his Victoria Cross and a silver plated revolver that had been given to him by the family of Commander Hay. Then, tragically, on 16 March, aged just fifty-six, he was drowned in the flooded Mikonui River.

Surgeon William Maillard was another winner of the Victoria Cross. Serving on the torpedo gunboat *Hazard*, launched in February 1894, he was thirty-five years old when Crete was occupied by the British in 1898 after a mob attacked the small force of soldiers at the Customs House in Candia. The British hospital at the other end of town was also attacked.

With no support coming from the Turkish force that was supposedly keeping order, the *Hazard* opened fire with her 4-inch guns – whereupon the mob went wild. Almost 1,000 women and children were killed or hurt and the *Hazard* had no option but to send a Naval Brigade ashore.

Screw Sloop *Harrier.*

The sloop *Harrier*, launched from the dockyard in 1831, served in many of the 'Little Wars' of Queen Victoria's reign. On 29 April 1864 Samuel Mitchell from the ship won the Victoria Cross during an action in the Maori Wars.

H.M.S. Hazard.

Another VC was won by Surgeon William Maillard whilst serving on the Pembroke Dock ship *Hazard* in an action on the coast of Crete.

Serving with the ship's Brigade, Maillard ran through a deluge of bullets to rescue a wounded sailor who had been hit trying to leave the boat. Maillard found he could hardly lift the man who was severely wounded and almost dead. Bullets passed through his coat and other clothing but he continued his efforts and, as a result, became the first naval medical officer to win the VC. He later became Staff Surgeon and died in retirement at Bournemouth in 1903.

By 1890 the Portuguese had begun making warlike moves along the Zambesi, hoping to establish a supply route into Central Africa. In an early version of what would now be called a 'retaliatory strike' the Pembroke Dock gunboats *Redbreast* and *Pigeon* were ordered into action. Together, they crossed the sand bar at the mouth of the river, their shallow draughts helping to ease their passage, and forced their way upstream.

The *Pigeon* then developed engine problems and was obliged to return to the coast but *Redbreast* continued on her journey and eventually broke out into open water. Sighting the gunboat, the Portuguese forces immediately surrendered and recognised British claims to the region. It was a small and seemingly slight action but it was typical of the type of duty gunboats were asked to carry out in those days.

Portugal featured heavily in the career of the sloop *Pelican*, launched from the yards on 7 March 1860. Sold to private buyers in 1867, she was renamed *Hawk*. She was then sold on again to the Portuguese navy. Now renamed *Infanta Dom Henrique*, she served mainly on the Angola station before being removed from the Portuguese navy list in 1879 and scrapped the following year.

The use of Naval Brigades became an increasing part of 'gunboat diplomacy' as the nineteenth century progressed. To give just one example, Pembroke Dock's first

The gunboat *Redbreast* which was active on the West African station, taking part in several campaigns along the rivers and shallow waters of the region.

Curacoa, a 31-gun frigate launched on 13 April 1854, was flagship of the Australian Station during the New Zealand Land Wars and supplied a Naval Brigade to help in the storming of the Maori fortress at Rangari. One officer and one sailor from the ship were killed during the operation.

Towards the end of the nineteenth century several Pembroke Dock vessels were also involved in fishery protection duties. Notable among these was the *Bullfrog*, a composite steam gunboat launched in February 1881. Stationed off the Canadian coast, the captain and crew of the *Bullfrog* had to follow a fine line between placating the local settlers and the French fishermen who claimed fishing rights and were increasingly flexing their muscles in the area.

Sometimes the actions they had to take were unpalatable. In 1887 Lieutenant Masterman of the *Bullfrog* wrote to a certain Mr Shearer, the owner of a lobster cannery on Kepal Island off Newfoundland, 'I have to inform you that you will continue working your factory next season at great risk.' Any complaint from the French, he went on to say, would result in the factory being suppressed. Conflict between the French and Canadian settlers/fishermen went on until 1904.

Opposite above: The use of Naval Brigades, sailors serving ashore as soldiers, increased as Victoria's reign and the expansion of the Empire ground on. This postcard view shows sailors at drill in front of their training ships, preparing for the only combat most of them would ever see – ashore.

Opposite middle: Members of a Naval Brigade practicing skirmishing, *c.* 1890

Opposite below: The gunboat *Bullfrog* served on the North American station and was heavily involved in fishery protection duties off the coast of Newfoundland.

The *Buzzard*, a steam sloop launched in 1849 but not commissioned until 1852, had a chequered career that included surveying work and anti-slavery patrols. The summer of 1854, while the Crimean War was still raging, found her on the coast of Nova Scotia and Newfoundland where, on 30 July, she was forced to fire one of her guns as a warning signal for French fishermen to leave Black Jake Cove.

Just a few days later, on 1 August, she stopped a French trawler laden with illegally caught fish. The French ship was brought alongside and the catch unceremoniously dumped overboard.

As the nineteenth century went on, anti-slavery operations became increasingly important for the navy. Slavery had been abolished in Britain but many other nations were still involved in the trade. By 1848 the Royal Navy had twenty-four vessels cruising off West Africa, nine off the Cape, twelve off Brazil and ten off the West Indies, all attempting to stop the slave traffic. The *Cleopatra*, launched on 28 April 1835, was one of these ships.

Armed with twenty-six guns of various calibre, the *Cleopatra* was a formidable opponent for any slaver and late in 1841 she duly stopped and captured the Spanish slave vessel *Segundo Rosario*. A total of 284 slaves were freed in the operation. On 12 April 1843 she took the slave brigantine *Prospero*. This time the slaver was carrying 444 slaves.

Not all of the *Cleopatra*'s interventions were uniformly successful, however. On 18 May 1846 she came across the Brazilian brig *Kentucky* in the Angozha River in Mozambique. The Brazilian vessel was clearly fitted out for the slave trade but before the *Cleopatra* could get men across, the *Kentucky* crew had fired their ship and escaped up river.

The illegal trade of 'blackbirding' – tricking people, or even kidnapping them, and then forcing them to work in industries like mining and on sugar cane plantations – became a growing problem in the Far East. In 1883 the gunboat *Swinger* was sent to the Australian Station with the express purpose of eliminating blackbirding.

A year later, in 1884, off the coast of New Guinea she fell in with a ship called the *Forest King*. On investigation it was found that sixty illegally taken islanders were being kept in the ship's hold. Lieutenant Marx, commanding the *Swinger*, told the Captain of the *Forest King* that he would be taken into port next day – if he tried to escape his ship would be sunk.

Later that night the quartermaster reported to Lt Marx that the crew of the *Forest King* seemed to be throwing things over the side. When Marx trained his binoculars on the ship he found that they were actually throwing their human cargo into the sea in order to get rid of incriminating evidence. Marx ordered his crew into the boats – many of them only half dressed – and they managed to rescue eighteen men from the water. He then boarded the *Forest King* and took her into Brisbane where, in due course, her captain was convicted of slave running not, as he deserved, cold blooded murder!

Interestingly, as the trial began Lt Marx was warned not to walk the streets of Brisbane or to allow his men to do the same, at least not in uniform. Apparently there was considerable vested interest in the blackbirding trade in the Brisbane area and feelings against the British ship ran high.

One Pembroke Dock ship in particular to achieve a degree of notoriety was the *Carysfort*, launched from the yards on 12 August 1836. A 26-gun sixth rate, she was in the Pacific when Lord George Paulet became Captain on 28 December 1841. Just

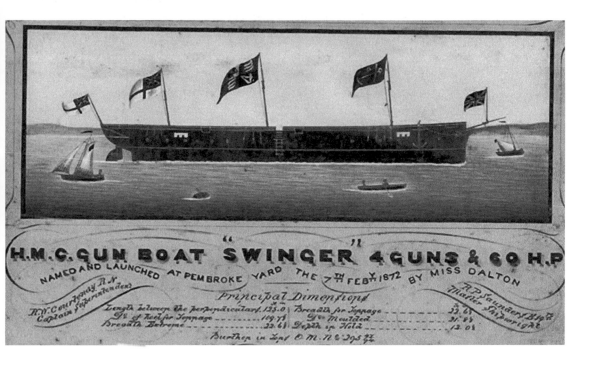

H.M.C. GUN BOAT "SWINGER" 4 GUNS & 60 H.P.

NAMED AND LAUNCHED AT PEMBROKE YARD THE 7TH FEBY 1872 BY MISS DALTON

Above: This print shows the launch of the Ariel-class gunboat *Swinger* at Pembroke Dock on 7 February 1872. Sent out to Australia, she was active in anti-slavery work, her commission from the Admiralty ordering her to eliminate the practice of 'blackbirding'– slavery by any other name.

Right: This *Illustrated London News* print shows a Royal Naval crew capturing a slaver off the coast of Africa. Eliminating slavery was a task to which the RN became more and more committed as the century passed.

over a year later he took control of the Government of Hawaii, then an independent state but with close connections to the nearby USA.

The Paulet Affair, as it was called, came about when Richard Charlton, British Consul on Hawaii since 1825, encountered the *Carysfort* off the coast of Mexico. Charlton told Paulet that British citizens on the islands were being denied their legal rights by the king and his dictatorial regime. When Admiral Thomas, the British commander in the Pacific, gave Paulet instructions to investigate, the die was set and Paulet seized his chance for glory.

Paulet did not just investigate, he deposed King Kamehameha, took control of the islands and set up a three-man government (including himself) to run the country. When American warships, now thoroughly alarmed at the course of events off the coast of the mainland USA, arrived in Hawaii, Paulet publicly burned the Hawaiian flag and announced that he would bombard Honolulu if there was any interference with his governance. Between February and July 1843 the tiny 26-gun vessel from Pembroke Dock sat in the harbour, Paulet clearly enjoying his moment of absolute power.

Eventually, Admiral Thomas restored the Hawaiian king and announced that Paulet had exceeded his authority. The status quo was re-established but for a while diplomatic tensions between the USA and Britain had run exceedingly high. And nobody doubted that Lord George Paulet needed only the slimmest of excuses to carry out his threat and open fire on Honolulu.

Soon after the restoration of the king things calmed down and the *Carysfort* returned to Britain. She had had an adventurous few months but just two years later she was laid up at Pembroke Dock, her home port, and duly scrapped.

When Jacky Fisher became First Sea Lord in October 1904 the age of gunboat diplomacy came to an abrupt end. Britain still needed to fly the flag and there were still colonial conflicts to sort out – just not with gunboats. They were, Fisher declared, 'Too weak to fight, too slow to run away.' And that spelled real trouble for the dockyard at Pembroke Dock.

Gunboats and small sloops were exactly what Pembroke Dock had specialised in for years. But Fisher wanted big gun ships like the *Dreadnought* and soon the 12-inch guns of the *Dreadnought* were superseded by the huge 15-inch weapons of the *Queen Elizabeth* class in a weapons or arms race that eventually culminated in the First World War. Pembroke Dockyard was not equipped to cope.

With Germany now seen as the main opponent in any future war, it was equally clear that naval installations like dockyards and ports needed to be situated along the east coast of Britain. Pembroke Dockyard, indeed all of Milford Haven, was in the wrong place.

The *Cockchafer* of 1881 might have been the yard's last composite gunboat but there were other vessels to build. For the moment questions about the Dockyard's future lay too far ahead to worry about and with the dawning of a new century hopes and dreams still ran high in the yards of Pembroke Dock.

12

Ships of Note – Success and Failure

Pembroke Dockyard produced many ships of note, some of which have already been mentioned – vessels like the *Iris* and *Mercury*, the first steel-hulled ships in the Royal Navy, and the *Duke of Wellington*, the largest wooden warship ever built. But there were many more.

The *Vesuvius*, launched on 29 March 1974, for example, can arguably be called the Royal Navy's first torpedo gunboat. Normally this recognition is afforded to the *Lightning* but *Vesuvius* was built with one submerged bow torpedo tube and, importantly, was launched three years before.

The *Vesuvius* held ten torpedoes in a forward compartment from which her single torpedo tube was operated. Her deep hull and low freeboard helped to make her engines as noiseless as possible and, as originally built, there was no funnel. The smoke from her engines – coke was burned rather than coal in an attempt to reduce the quantities of smoke – was released from vents along her side. The aim behind this revolutionary design was to help the *Vesuvius* carry out unseen attacks on enemy shipping but she made only a disappointing 9.4 knots in her sea trials.

With Admiralty thinking polarised on speed, the *Vesuvius* was never going to enjoy a particularly successful career. Soon after her launch she was given a tall funnel, thus making it easier to raise steam. Never widely used, she was soon relegated to experimental and instructional work with HMS *Vernon*, the navy's torpedo school.

The *Vanguard*, launched on 25 August 1835, was known as a Symondite. Designed by Sir William Symonds, she was the first ship in a class of eleven. The Symondites were based on an American idea where the basic shape of the ship conformed to a pre-constructed frame. Once the original frame had been built it could be copied and then stored for years before being put into use.

The *Vanguard* was laid down in May 1833 and it needed just sixty skilled shipwrights, working solidly for sixteen weeks, to set up the frame. At the time of her launch she was the broadest ship ever built for the navy, nearly 4,000 loads of timber being used in her construction. She, like all of the Symondites, was designed to be fast and, when commissioned, she was indeed renowned as the fastest ship in the Mediterranean Fleet.

Along with the *Iris*, the *Mercury*, launched at Pembroke Dock in 1878, was the Navy's first steel vessel, a revolutionary new ship. She was one of many successful and important ships of note to come out of the Welsh yards, being for a while the fastest ship in the navy.

Her wide beam was supposed to provide stability but, in practice, like all the ships of her class, the *Vanguard* rolled heavily. This, unfortunately, made what was otherwise a revolutionary vessel a rather poor gun platform. Renamed *Ajax* in 1867 to allow a newer ship to take the name *Vanguard*, she was broken up in 1875.

The *Cylops* and *Gorgon* have already been mentioned, the first steam vessels over 1,000 tons. Yet they both have another claim to fame. The two ships helped to lay the first Atlantic telegraph cable in 1857, a mammoth undertaking and one that achieved considerable publicity at the time. It really was the start of a new age and two Pembroke Dock ships were there at the very beginning.

One of the most successful of all Pembroke Dock ships was the battleship *Collingwood* of 1882. Sir William Houston, Controller of the Navy, recommended that she be equipped with new model 12-inch guns, breech loaders mounted in barbettes rather than turrets. This would, he said, extend the elevation and depression of the gun barrels.

With an armour belt of between eight and eighteen inches of thickness (the greater thickness of armour being amidships, protecting the ship's engines and communication systems), the ends of the *Collingwood*'s armour belt were closed by bulkheads sixteen inches thick.

She was a superb design, apart from a low freeboard that did somewhat restrict her mobility in anything other than a moderate sea. She was, however, exceedingly fast, being the first British battleship to achieve a speed of over 16 knots under steam. So successful was this mighty warship that all succeeding battleships built for the Royal Navy until the launch of the *Dreadnought* in 1905, were really just improvements and modifications on the *Collingwood*'s design.

Above: The *Gorgon* was one of Pembroke Dock's first steam vessels. Considered something of an unlucky ship – her name spelled backwards read 'No Grog'– she later went on to help lay the first transatlantic telegraph cable.

Right: One of the most successful ships ever launched from Pembroke Dock, the *Collingwood* (1882) provided a blueprint for almost all subsequent battleships up to the arrival of the *Dreadnought* in 1906.

Gun turrets or barbettes? It was a question that occupied the minds of most naval architects during the nineteenth century. This photograph shows the open barbettes of a British battleship at the end of the 1880s.

The *Edinburgh* of 1882 (beating the *Collingwood* into the water by a few months) was both a 'first' and a 'last.' Either way she was a vessel of note. She was the first RN battleship to carry a main armament of breech loading guns and also the first to have compound, rather than iron, armour plating. She was also the last of the great Victorian citadel ships.

The battleship *Renown*, launched on 8 May 1895, was another Pembroke Dock ship of some note, not so much because of her design – although she was actually the first British battleship to be given all steel armour plating – but because of how she was used. Originally built to lead cruiser squadrons in colonial regions, cruiser design and speed soon outstripped that of the lightly armed *Renown*. But Jacky Fisher fell in love with her, took her with him to his new command in the Mediterranean and attracted much criticism because of it.

Prince Louis of Battenberg, then Assistant of Naval Intelligence, was clear that the *Renown* had no right to act as Fisher's flagship. She was, he believed, under-gunned and too slow for such a role. As he said at the time:

> We want the biggest and best in the Mediterranean: JF, of course, won't part with his 'yacht' but it is quite wrong.[26]

Fisher's departure from Malta when he relinquished his command in 1902 was a bravura performance. The *Renown* steamed out of the Grand Harbour at 16 knots, as

Designed to operate with cruiser squadrons, HMS *Renown* became the favourite ship of Jacky Fisher and later went on to take members of the Royal family on cruises across the world.

fast as any gunboat – Jacky clearly making a point to his critics – and with her guns firing a salute to the Governor of the island. As she went, the *Renown* flew the largest Admiral's flag anybody had ever seen.[27]

The *Shannon* of 1875 was the first British armoured cruiser. Never totally successful, she had an experimental hull, giving her a foot wider beam than other cruisers but a shallower draught. The modified hull was, ultimately, a failure as the *Shannon* failed to reach over 22 knots on her trials.

Originally designed with short funnels, thanks to Jacky Fisher's instructions, these were later raised by fifteen feet as smoke from her stacks caused major observation problems.

The *Shannon* was in Russia at the end of the First World War, replacing the *Cochrane* on duty at Murmansk and then Archangel. She returned to the Home Fleet at the end of 1918 and was sold for scrap in 1922.

The *Boadicea*, launched in 1908, was one of several light or scout cruisers built in the yards following the end of the gunboat period. A beautiful looking ship, she was unique at the time in having a platform in front of her bridge – on which her forward gun was mounted.

Her sister ship, the *Blonde*, launched a few years later, was one of the first cruisers to carry 21-inch torpedoes. The tubes for these were mounted between the second and third funnels, on either beam. *Boadicea*, *Bellona* and *Blanche* – all Pembroke Dock ships – were at Jutland in 1916 but the *Blonde* missed out on the greatest battle of the war.

Two of Pembroke Dock's best-known ships are shown in this photograph. The *Thunderer*, then serving as guard ship for the dockyard is moored mid-stream while the giant *Hannibal* sits, partially completed, off Hobbs Point fitting out berth.

HMS *Ajax*, launched in 1880, was one of the least successful of all Pembroke Dock ships. She rolled incessantly and was anything but a stable gun platform.

Dignitaries descending from the podium after a launch at Pembroke Dockyard – the crowd of local people (always admitted to the yards to watch a launch) gaze on in admiration.

HMS *Blonde*, one of the fast light cruisers in which the dockyard came to specialise, is shown here alongside Carr Jetty after her launch in 1910.

13
Punishments

Life in the Georgian and Victorian navy was incredibly hard and punishment for crimes or even non-compliance with orders was both swift and brutal.

For much of the nineteenth century captains on board Royal Navy ships literally held the power of life and death over their sailors even though the more odious punishments such as keel hauling and flogging round the fleet had been ended in the middle years of the eighteenth century.

Flogging, on the whim or, if the sailors were lucky, on the judgement of the captain, was a different matter. It was, thought those in positions of power, the only way to avoid mutiny, desertion and open rebellion – a reasonable enough assumption when almost half of the ordinary seamen on board the navy's warships did not want to be there and were only serving because they had been caught up by the press gang.

Many of these pressed men were merchant sailors, taken from their vessels on their way into port, usually at the end of long and hazardous voyages to and from places like China and India. Others were landsmen with little or no experience of the sea, although it has to be stated that there were far less of these than popular myth allows.

The end of impressment did not happen overnight. It was only the establishment, in the 1860s, of a Continuous Service Scheme for seamen and, a few years later, the creation of a formal Naval Reserve that really spelled the end of the press gang. Severe punishments such as flogging also began to decline in use at the same time – decline but not disappear:

> We know that 2,007 men were flogged in 1839 but only 860 in 1847. However, even in 1852 there were ships where it was a weekly, if no longer daily occurrence.[28]

Flogging had been restricted to just twelve cuts by the Colonial Naval regulations of 1775 but this was a restriction that was often overlooked by ship's captains. It was eventually suspended in the peace time navy in 1871 (for times of war the punishment was retained until 1879) and, thereafter, was never resumed. Technically, however, flogging was still an available deterrent and the punishment was not removed from the statute books until 1947.

Flogging on the quarterdeck, before the assembled crew – an early print by the artist George Cruikshank in 1826.

As late as 1880 a marine on board the gunboat *Mosquito*, launched from Pembroke Dock on 9 December 1871, was sentenced to twenty-five lashes with the cat o' nine tails – nine leather thongs each with a knot at the end – to be followed by two years of prison with hard labour. The Admiralty, on hearing of the captain's sentence on the marine, promptly intervened. The flogging was cancelled but the two year prison sentence was retained.

Several other Pembroke Dock ships had interesting connections to naval punishments. Notable among these was the *Vanguard*. On the night of 30 January 1838 the ship's First Lieutenant ordered the Assistant Surgeon to stomach pump a drunken seaman. Robert Scott, the Assistant Surgeon in question, disagreed but the No. 1 ordered him to carry out the treatment – as a punishment and as a deterrent for the man in question.

Shortly afterwards Scott was ordered to repeat the process with another seaman and was threatened with court martial when he tried to complain to the captain. It was only when the matter became known and talked about in the fleet that the Admiralty issued an order banning the use of stomach pumping as a punishment.

The *Egeria*, a four-gunned sloop launched in November 1873, had an adventurous life, notably taking part in a campaign in what is now known as Malaysia to avenge the murder of the British Resident, Mr James Birch. A Naval Brigade was sent ashore while the *Egeria* herself blockaded the Peak River. Guns and ammunition were recovered but the murderers were never caught.

A near mutiny took place on board the gunboat *Egeria* while she was surveying the coast of Australia in 1886.

More interestingly, perhaps, while she was surveying the Australian coast one of her sailors and a Petty Officer were tried for mutiny and for disobeying orders. Flogging was no longer an option but the two men were sentenced to five years penal servitude. Five other sailors were tried for disobedience and sentenced to terms of between one year and six months in prison. The ship's captain, Pelham Aldrich, clearly ran a hard ship and the rigors of life on the hot, humid Australian coast had proved too much for the sailors.

The battleship *Caesar*, of Betty Foggy fame, became the centre of controversy in July 1859 while she was undergoing a refit at Devonport. According to a report in *The Times* a sailor by the name of William Stephenson attempted to persuade the *Caesar*'s crew to mutiny or, at the very least, be insubordinate. His motive behind this was never clear but Stephenson then made things a whole lot worse by assaulting Mr Grigg, the ship's bosun.

Stephenson was arrested, tried and sentenced to fifty lashes. He was lucky. Fifty years before he could easily have been hanged.

On the day the punishment was to be carried out, Stephenson was brought out to the *Caesar* from his prison cell at 6.00 a.m. His coat was stripped from his back and, in the time-honoured way, he was lashed to a grating on the deck.

Dockyard workers (artisans, as *The Times* reporter who witnessed the event called them) were due to start their shifts at 7.00 a.m. but were delayed from coming on

HMS *Caesar* was used to controversy, thanks to a supposed cursing on her launching day. A flogging on board the ship almost caused a major riot at Devonport in 1859.

board as there were to be no civilian witnesses to the punishment. Not to be put off, the workers flocked to high ground overlooking the anchorage and onto a Turkish ship called the *Shadia*, also undergoing repairs and moored close to the *Caesar*, to watch the event. They crowded the decks and the portholes of the Turkish ship.

Bosun Grigg was given the 'honour' of taking the first dozen strokes. Clearly enjoying his revenge, the Bosun spat on his hands and attacked Stephenson's naked back with relish. Then his assistants took over. The dockyard workers and Turkish sailors hissed and groaned at every cry the prisoner uttered.

Infuriated by the reaction, Captain Mason of the *Caesar* sent a party of officers and marines onto the *Shadia* in an attempt to disperse the watchers and arrest the ringleaders. Things did not go quite the way Mason had planned, however. There were a number of scuffles, during which one of the officers, Lieutenant Dickson, was knocked to the deck. Police were called to reinforce the party from the *Caesar* and, after a while, order was restored. In the wake of the incident several dockyard workers were arrested and suspended from their jobs. According to *The Times* it was over fifty years since a punishment like this had been inflicted on any ship moored in Devonport Dockyard.

Several Pembroke Dock vessels ended their lives as prison hulks or police ships where punishment of various types would have been given out on a regular basis. Although flogging had been effectively ended in the 1870s, the ruling did not apply to naval prisons, where the lash was used for many years to come.

Left: Sailors in their distinctive hats and jumpers, *c.* 1850

Below: After December 1860, keeping order in Pembroke Dockyard, as in all Royal Naval yards, became the responsibility of the Metropolitan Police. The establishment originally consisted of one Superintendent, two inspectors, five sergeants and twenty-six constables. They also had to man the dockyard fire engine, as this photograph clearly shows.

A landscape view of Pembroke Dockyard, showing the giant building sheds, at the beginning of the twentieth century.

The *Helena* of 1843 was just one Pembroke Dock ship to end this way. She became a police hulk in 1863, a floating chapel in 1868, then a police hulk again in 1883. Finally she was converted into the harbour police ship at Chatham, a role she fulfilled until 1921.

The *Penelope*, the last small ironclad built for the navy, in 1867, was a poor seaboat, probably because of her excessively shallow draught. She apparently drifted to windward on a regular basis, which did not make her an easy vessel to manoeuvre. She was, incidentally, the first British capital ship to be fitted with a washroom – for officers, naturally.

She served largely in the Mediterranean and took part in the bombardment of Alexandria on 11 July 1882. When Admiral Seymour discovered that rebel forces were strengthening the fortifications of Alexandria he took his ships inshore to bombard the port. *Penelope* was so close inshore that she was hit several times by shore batteries, one of her eight 8-inch guns being destroyed by a direct hit during the action.

Paid off in 1887, the *Penelope* was refitted and sent to Simonstown in South Africa where, initially, she became the harbour receiving ship. In 1897, however, she was converted into a prison ship for the port and the immediate area. She remained in this role until she was finally broken up in 1912.

The ships of Pembroke Dockyard were no different from any others in the navy. Their officers were not particularly brutal or insensitive – at least, not more than any other naval officer of the time – but the punishments handed out on board these ships reflect the harsh reality of life afloat. They are just one more example of Pembroke Dock ships being in the forefront of naval life during the nineteenth century.

14
Pre-Dreadnoughts

By the beginning of the 1880s Pembroke Dockyard, although specialising in gunboats and similar small craft, had also produced a regular stream of large battleships. Conditions at the yard may not have been perfect for the construction of such craft but the workforce exceeded all expectations and produced vessels of stunning quality and size.

Looking back at the massive pre-Dreadnoughts produced by Pembroke Dockyard in the closing years of the nineteenth century, vessels such as the *Repulse* and *Hannibal*, it is quite amazing to think that they were fitted out at the tiny jetty of Hobbs Point, a landing stage that these days would be struggling to hold twenty or thirty cars.

The *Howe*, launched on 28 April 1885, was the first true pre-Dreadnought battleship to be built in the yards although ships like the *Edinburgh* and *Collingwood* might, arguably, also have a claim to the title.

The essential prerequisites for a pre-Dreadnought battleship, however, included a total lack of sails, turrets and breech loading main armament arranged on a fore and aft basis, rapid firing smaller weapons to defend against torpedo boat attack, steel based armour plating and triple expansion engines. The Admiral Class, of which *Howe* was one of the earliest examples, were the first capital ships to have every single one of these qualities.[29]

The *Howe* was supposed to be equipped with four 13.5-inch guns, new weapons for the Ordnance, fitted in barbettes without shields or hoods. But delays in casting the guns meant that by 1890 – five years after her launch – she still had only two of her main weapons installed. Once the guns were finally fitted she was sent to join the Mediterranean Fleet where, on 2 November 1892, she grounded on Ferrol Rock and was not freed until 30 March the following year. In 1896 the *Howe* was relegated to the position of port guardship at Queenstown in Ireland. She was eventually broken up in 1910.

The *Anson* of February 1886 was the last of the Admiral Class battleships. At 330 feet in length she was a massive ship, her four 13.5-inch guns and secondary armament (six 6-inch and smaller) being designed to match current French capital ships. As with the *Howe*, there were delays in producing her new guns and the *Anson* lay for two years at Portsmouth, waiting for her weaponry. The *Anson* was paid off

Together with her sister ship *Devastation*, the *Thunderer* was the second mastless capital ship in the navy. She was, for a time, the most powerful ship afloat.

Designed to transit the Suez Canal, the *Edinburgh* was launched on 18 March 1882. Her shallow draught caused many problems.

into the Reserve in May 1904, just prior to the *Dreadnought* coming into service, and was sold for scrapping in 1909.

Launched two years after the *Anson*, on 27 March 1888, the *Nile* was the last British battleship with a single citadel amidships. All subsequent battleships were given two citadels, fore and aft. She was also the first British capital ship to mount a secondary armament of quick firing guns where charge and shell were combined in one cartridge and loaded into the breach as a single unit.

The *Nile* served mainly in the Mediterranean but in January 1898 she became the guardship at Devonport. She then moved to the Reserve before being sold for scrap on 9 July 1912.

When the *Repulse* was launched on 27 February 1892, thousands of excursionists came swooping into Pembroke Dock to witness the event, many of them from as far away as Swansea and Cardiff. This Royal Sovereign class battleship was 410 feet in length with a beam of 75 feet. Like *Anson* and *Nile* she was armed with 13.5-inch guns and was capable of a top speed of 17 knots.

However, like all of her class, due to her high freeboard the *Repulse* rolled heavily, so much so that all ships in the class were nicknamed 'The rolling Ressies.' In an

The *Repulse*, shown alongside the giant building sheds. Thousands came to Pembroke Dock to see her launch in February 1892.

The largest vessel ever built at Pembroke Dock, the *Hannibal* was the last British battleship to have her funnels side by side.

attempt to solve the problem, *Repulse* was equipped with experimental bilge keels, a solution that seemed to work.

The Royal Sovereign class vessels were the front line battleships of the Royal Navy until the advent of the *Dreadnought* in 1906. The *Repulse* served in home waters and was part of the squadron that visited Germany for the opening of the Kaiser Wilhelm Canal. On 26 June 1897 she was also one of dozens of ships present in the Fleet Review for Victoria's Diamond Jubilee. She was eventually scrapped in July 1911.

At 14,900 tons, the *Hannibal* was the biggest and last battleship to be built at Pembroke Dock, sliding into the waters of the Haven on 28 April 1896. A Majestic-Class battleship, she and the rest of her class were the last British battleships to have their funnels side by side, a fore and aft alignment being adopted on all subsequent capital ships.

In 1906 she was one of six battleships in the Channel Fleet when the Russian Admiral Zinovi Petrovitch Rozhestvensky, on his way to eventual destruction at the hands of the Japanese in the Battle of Tsushima, mistakenly opened fire on British trawlers in the North Sea, believing them to be Japanese torpedo boats. Public opinion was outraged and the British demanded recompense.

It was a tense moment. 'Situation critical', signaled Admiral Charles Beresford of the Channel Fleet, flying his flag in the *Caesar*. Gibraltar was put on a war footing and, for a while, it really did appear as if Britain and Russia might come to blows. By the evening of 26 October, Beresford had twenty-eight battleships and cruisers waiting for

Roshestvensky in the Western Approaches but, in the end, diplomacy averted conflict and the Russians steamed on to their doom.[30]

Hannibal was twice involved in serous collisions, occasions when she escaped serious damage but when the other vessels were lucky to get away without sinking. The first was with the battleship *Prince George* off Ferrol in October 1903, the second with a small gunboat on 29 October 1909. The *Hannibal* became guardship at Scapa Flow, home of the Grand Fleet, in August 1914 and the following year, with her main armament removed, she served as a troop ship during the Gallipoli Campaign. In November 1915 she became a depot ship at Alexandria and was duly sold and scrapped in Italy in 1920.

Scrapping was a natural fate for most Pembroke Dock ships but some, like the *Empress of India*, launched in May 1891, met a more spectacular end. She had enjoyed an adventurous career that included being the flagship of the Channel Fleet, taking part in the Diamond Jubilee Review of 1897 and being part of the blockading squadron off Crete during the Greco-Turkish rising in 1898. On 30 April 1906 she collided with the submarine A19 in Plymouth Sound, luckily without serious damage to either vessel.

The pre-dreadnought *Empress of India*, launched in 1891, is shown here in dry dock during a refit at Malta, *c.* 1898. The ship was undoubtedly powerful but with Britain not having fought a major sea war since the actions in the Crimea, more emphasis was placed on design and decoration than was strictly necessary.

The *Empress of India* ended her days as a target vessel for other ships, being sunk in Lyme Regis Bay in 1913.

Paid off in 1912, the *Empress of India* became a target ship when, on 4 November 1913, she was moored in Lyme Regis Bay and seven battleships and numerous cruisers opened fire on her. Within a short space of time she was blazing furiously and was down by the stern. At 18.30 in the evening she slipped slowly beneath the waves, having received forty-four 12-inch and 13-inch hits from the attacking force.

Until the advent of oil burning engines, a regular and sufficient supply of coal was the most important factor in all naval dispositions. Every navy in the world needed coal for fuel but it was heavy, unwieldy to manage and enormously time consuming to load onto the ships. Officers might have tried to insert a 'competitive' edge to the coaling process, taking pride in being faster than other ships, but there was no denying the back-breaking nature of the job.

Coaling from colliers in Milford Haven in 1898 the *Hannibal* shipped an average of 91 tons per hour, the *Repulse* managing just 80 tons.[31] Taking on coal in a safe anchorage like Milford Haven was one thing; doing it in potentially hostile waters was a different matter:

> For nations like Britain, with widely scattered interests to protect, the only answer was to build up numerous coaling stations all over the world.[32]

In order to protect these coaling stations and the trade routes that kept the Empire supplied, Britain needed a fleet of fast, well armed ships that could respond to a crisis quickly and effectively – the cruiser concept was born. In the closing years of the nineteenth and in the early twentieth centuries Pembroke Dockyard built many such ships.

Coaling was perhaps the most demanding but essential task ever endured by sailors. This shows a coaling lighter alongside a battleship of the Channel Fleet, *c.* 1898.

Cruisers of the pre-dreadnought era tended to fall into two distinct classes. Protected cruisers were built without side armour, making them wide open to torpedo attack, while armoured cruisers were exactly the opposite, having heavy side protection but decks that were open to high, plunging shot – weaknesses that became only too apparent when war broke out in 1914.[33]

With the rapid development of the destroyer concept, a new type of cruiser became necessary at the beginning of the twentieth century. The navy now needed ships that were light and quick enough to operate in conjunction with the destroyers that were already providing a sighting screen for any battle fleet. And once again Pembroke Dock proved the ideal place to build these light and scout cruisers. Vessels such as the *Boadecia*, *Bellona*, *Blonde* and *Blanche* soon became a staple diet of the building sheds at Pembroke Dock.

At 529 feet, the armoured cruiser *Drake*, launched on 5 March 1901, was the longest vessel ever built at Pembroke Dock. An excess of £22,000 was incurred in her construction, the cost of labour far exceeding the original estimate. *The Times* commented, 'A good deal of the excess is accounted for by the lack of facilities for completing large ships at the dockyard' and, in consequence of such criticism, Carr

Right: The cruiser *Essex* off Hobbs Point.

Below: The light cruiser *Boadicea* leaves the slipway, 14 May 1908.

Dignitaries and dockyard officers might stand idly and happily on the bridge of the *Bellona* during her launch on 20 March 1909, but for the workman in the foreground of the photograph there is still work to be done.

Jetty within the confines of the dockyard was finally built as an extra fitting out berth.[34]

Quite apart from limited protection, the *Duke of Edinburgh*, launched 14 January 1904, had other serious design flaws. Her supplementary 6-inch gun battery was mounted too low to the waterline and was therefore unusable in anything like a heavy sea. It was not until the outbreak of the First World War that alterations were finally made. She also carried twenty 3-pdr guns but these were too small to be much use against torpedo boat or destroyer attacks.

Learning from the mistake, the ships of the *Warrior* class – only one, the *Warrior* herself, being built at Pembroke Dock – underwent redesign to mount the secondary armament of 7.5-inch guns in turrets on the upper deck. With fire control platforms, from which the guns were directed, in the masts these were excellent sea boats.

As the twentieth century progressed, ship building at Pembroke Dock continued. Interestingly, however, in the 1909 Naval Estimates five protected cruisers (the Bristol Class) were proposed – none of them were to be built at Pembroke Dock. Light cruisers such as the *Active* and *Amphion* were. The yards, it seemed, had already been relegated to the 'Light Cruiser Class.' If the workmen at Pembroke Dock noticed or realised, they said nothing.

The town and the yards celebrated their centenary in the summer of 1914, little knowing that death, destruction and, eventually, the demise of the dockyard itself were hovering just over the horizon.

The launch of the *Duke of Edinburgh* in January 1904. She was the only ship in the 1st Cruiser Squadron to avoid destruction at the Battle of Jutland.

A torpedo boat squadron and escorting light cruiser lie off the dockyard in the early years of the twentieth century. The cruiser moored to Carr Jetty in the background is probably the *Warrior*, which was then being fitted out in the yards.

15

The First World War

Britain went to war with Germany on 4 August 1914. Within twenty-four hours Pembroke Dock had suffered its first casualty when the cruiser *Amphion* was mined in the North Sea. She was not just the first Pembroke Dock victim of the war – she was also the first Royal Naval loss.

Launched on 4 December 1911, the *Amphion* was a fast scout cruiser, designed to work with the destroyers that now operated either as fleet escorts or as independent attack craft. On 5 August the *Amphion*, under the command of Captain Cecil H. Fox, was at sea with the destroyers of the 3rd Flotilla where they were engaged in a sweep across the North Sea towards Heligoland Bight.

The former Hamburg-Holland ferry boat *Königin Luise* had left Germany the day before, her task to lay mines off the Thames Estuary. Early in the morning of 5 August she was spotted by the destroyers and two of them, the *Lance* and *Landrail*, immediately gave chase and opened fire. The destroyers were quickly joined by the *Amphion*, a ship that had recently won the fleet gunnery prize. The *Königin Luise* had no chance and was hit several times before rolling over onto her side and sinking. Forty-six of her crew of over 100 were saved.

At that moment another ship suddenly hove into view. This was the *St Petersburg*, a passenger vessel carrying the German ambassador back home. The destroyers pressed in to attack but as the *St Petersburg* had diplomatic immunity, Captain Fox signalled them to break off the action. When they did not respond he was forced to put the *Amphion* between them and the German vessel.

And then came disaster. At 06.45 the *Amphion* struck one of the mines recently laid by the *Königin Luise*. The explosion broke the ship's back and virtually destroyed the bridge. All of the forward gun crew were killed and most of those on the bridge were badly burned. A large number of the crew were at breakfast, where many were killed before they knew what was happening – along with nineteen of the German survivors so recently pulled from the water.

With the *Amphion* down by the bows and with fires raging in the forward part of the vessel, Captain Fox ordered Abandon Ship. Within twenty minutes everyone was on board the destroyers – including Midshipman E. F. Fegan, who would later win

The launch of the cruiser *Amphion* in 1911.

An artist's impression of the incident that led to the destruction of the '*Amphion*, the first British loss of the Great War,' on 5 August 1914. The minelayer *Königen Luise* lies crippled and sinking, surrounded by destroyers. A few hours later the *Amphion* would follow her to the bottom.

a posthumous Victoria Cross in the Second World War as the Captain of the armed merchant cruiser *Jervis Bay*.

Unfortunately, the *Amphion* still had way on, even though her engines were stopped. Slowly turning in a wide circle, she ran full tilt into another recently laid mine and this time her magazine detonated. There was a huge explosion and the ship

The *Drake*, one of the most photographed ships in the Royal Navy – presumably because of her name. The longest ship ever launched from Pembroke Dockyard, she was torpedoed and sunk on 2 October 1917.

sank at exactly 07.02. The *Amphion* lost one officer and 150 men in the action. With the war only thirty-two hours old, the incident inflicted both the first German and the first British naval losses of the war.

The *Amphion* was only the first. In total, seven Pembroke Dock ships were sunk during the course of the war. The cruiser *Drake*, once commanded by no less a person than John Jellicoe, later the commander of the Grand Fleet at Jutland, was torpedoed by U79 in Rathlin Sound on 2 October 1917. Eighteen men were killed, all of them in boiler room number two where the torpedo struck.

The *Nottingham*, launched only in 1913, was another submarine victim. She had previously taken part in the Battle of Heligoland Bight and the Dogger Bank action and at Jutland she was attached to the 2nd Light Cruiser Squadron. On 19 August 1916, while engaged in a sweep of the North Sea, she was suddenly struck by two torpedoes fired by U52. The *Nottingham* was 120 miles south of the Firth of Forth and there was a heavy mist across the area. It did not help her.

Twenty five minutes later, as the crew began to Abandon Ship, *Nottingham* was struck by a third torpedo. She sank at 07.10, just over an hour after she was first hit. Thankfully, there were only very few casualties.

The *Hazard* was launched in 1894 as a Dryad-Class torpedo gunboat. In 1901 she was converted into a submarine depot ship, one of the first in the Royal Navy, and on 2 February 1912 she somehow managed to collide with one of her own charges, the submarine A3. Four men on the submarine were drowned; there were no casualties on the *Hazard*.

The torpedo gunboat *Hazard* was launched in 1894 but was then converted into a submarine depot ship. She was lost in a collision in the English Channel in 1918.

In a moment of supreme poetic justice, the *Hazard* herself was later sunk in a collision. On 28 January 1918 she fell foul of the larger hospital ship *Western Australia* while on duty in the English Channel and went quickly to the bottom.

Pembroke Dock built five submarines during the war years, the J3 and J4 in 1916 and the H51, H52 and L10 in 1918. Of these, L10 was sunk by a German destroyer off Texel in 1918. Prior to this, during her diving trials off St Ann's Head in 1916 she failed to surface after touching the sea bed. The fault was eventually located and after several hours the submarine rose to the surface, much to the relief of the dockyard officials and workmen still on board.

Of the other submarines, J3 and J4 – for a brief while the fastest submarines in the navy – were transferred to the Royal Australian Navy in 1919. The J3 was scuttled at Swan Island in 1926 after coming out of service while the J4 sank at her moorings on 10 July 1924. Later raised from the sea bed, she was scuttled off Port Phillip Heads in what was known as 'the ships graveyard'. Her wreck still lies on the bottom, where it is supposed to provide good quality diving.

Pembroke Dockyard continued to build ships throughout the war but there were also many cancelled orders, particularly of submarines. During this time, as well as the regular flow of cruisers and submarines, the yards also produced the Royal Fleet Auxilliary tanker *Turmoil*. This experimental ship, launched in March 1917, was mechanically unsatisfactory. Part of the problem lay in the fact that her original engines were removed and placed in the monitors *Marshal Soult* and *Marshal Ney*, the replacement engines being under powered and of poor quality.

The J3 was one of five submarines built at Pembroke Dockyard. Others were planned but the orders were cancelled before they were laid down.

The submarine H52 was one of the last vessels built at Pembroke Dockyard, being launched just as the war was ending.

The yards had already launched one RFA tanker, the *Trefoil*, in 1913 – another vessel that lost her engines to the monitors – and was later to produce one more, the last Pembroke Dock ship to be built, the *Oleander*. The *Turmoil* spent most of the war at Devonport but in July 1919 she was sent to Biorko Sound in the Baltic as part of the support fleet for the White Russian armies. By 1925, however, she was laid up at Rosyth as being 'mechanically unsound' and was sold out of the navy in June 1935. The *Trefoil* was sold at the same time.

The cruiser *Cornwall* which played an active role in the destruction of the German fleet at the Battle of the Falkland Islands.

The cruiser *Duke of Edinburgh*, launched in 1904, was in action early in the war, capturing the German steamer *Altair* in the Red Sea at the end of August 1914. Two months later she was bombarding Turkish positions at Sheikh Sa'id in Southern Arabia. After surviving the carnage of Jutland she spent the rest of the war on transatlantic convoy duties.

The cruiser *Fearless*, launched in October 1913, started the war as Leader of the 1st Destroyer Flotilla in Harwich. In 1916 she became Leader of the 12th Submarine Flotilla, attached to the Grand Fleet, and in January 1918 accidentally rammed and sank K17, one of the new steam-powered K-Class submarines from her Flotilla.

Another Pembroke Dock cruiser, the *Cornwall*, launched on 29 October 1902, was also involved during the early stages of the conflict. August 1914 saw her off the west coast of Africa, intercepting German merchant shipping. She then became part of the squadron, commanded by Vice Admiral Doveton Sturdee, sent to the southern Atlantic to avenge the defeat of Christopher Craddock at the Battle of Coronel.

At the ensuing Battle of the Falkland Islands, the German fleet under Admiral von Spee was utterly destroyed, the armoured cruisers *Scharnhorst* and *Gneisenau* being pummeled by the guns of the British battlecruisers and only the light cruiser *Dresden* managing to escape. The *Cornwall* trained her guns against the *Leipzig*, quickly sending the German cruiser to the bottom.

After the battle, the *Cornwall* moved back to Africa where, in 1915, she became part of the blockading squadron keeping the German raider *Königsberg* holed up in the Rufigi Delta. A period on the China Station was followed by convoy duties in the Atlantic.

The other County Class cruiser built at Pembroke Dock was the *Essex*, launched in 1903. Unlike the *Cornwall* she had a relatively quiet war, starting with the 4th Cruiser Squadron in 1914 and being converted into a Destroyer Depot Ship in 1916. She was sold out of the navy in 1921.

Many Pembroke Dock ships served at the Battle of Jutland in May 1916, the only time that the British Grand Fleet and the German High Seas Fleet came face to face during the entire war.

The *Warrior*, *Defence* and *Duke of Edinburgh* (together with the *Black Prince*) made up the 1st Cruiser Squadron under Rear Admiral Sir Robert Arbuthnot, who flew his flag in *Defence*. Shortly after 18.00 hours on 31 May, when the battle had really only just begun, the 1st Cruiser Squadron was chasing a group of German scouts. Suddenly, out of the haze, loomed the battleships and battle cruisers of Admiral Hipper's 3rd Battle Squadron.

Hopelessly outnumbered and out gunned, Arbuthnot made to turn away. It was too late. The German capital ships opened fire and at 18.15 hours the *Defence* was hit by an enemy salvo. A gigantic flame shot up from abaft of her rear turret and the ship seemed to stagger and heel over. She quickly righted herself and continued on her course. She was immediately hit by a second salvo, this time between the forward funnel and turret. A huge cloud of black smoke engulfed the ship. When it cleared, the *Defence* had gone, taking Admiral Arbuthnot and nearly 900 men with her.

The *Warrior* was also hit by heavy 15-inch shells from the German battle cruisers and lost steam from her engines. She was soon on fire, listing sharply to port. The end would have come immediately had not the British battleship *Warspite* suddenly hove into view and the German ships veered away. As it was, the *Warrior* was gravely wounded.

German shells exploding around British warships.

The 1st Cruiser Squadron off the Nore in 1913. The flagship *Defence* and the *Warrior* were later sunk at Jutland.

A close up of the hull and secondary armament of the *Defence* shortly after completion.

As originally built the 6-inch secondary armament of the *Duke of Edinburgh* was sited too close to the waterline. In the early years of the war, these guns were removed from the lower casements and re-mounted on the upper deck. This shows her in a heavy sea, after the alterations had been made.

Beautiful to look at but doomed once she came under the guns of German battleships at Jutland, the *Warrior* is shown here just before war broke out.

Taken in tow by a seaplane carrier, to begin with there was every hope that the *Warrior* could be saved. But during the night of 31 May/1 June the weather deteriorated and the ship's stern sank lower and lower into the waves. Eventually, the seaplane carrier came alongside and took off all survivors. Soon afterwards the *Warrior* sank.

In the unequal contest between the British cruisers and the German battleships, the *Black Prince* was also sunk. Only the Pembroke Dock-built *Duke of Edinburgh* managed to escape destruction.

16

Decline and Fall

In Pembroke Dock, just like every other community in Britain, news of the Armistice on 11 November 1918 was received with rapturous joy. Ships in Milford Haven sounded their sirens and the guns from the Defensible Barracks above the town were fired in celebration. The dockyard shut up shop for the day and people thronged the streets, singing and dancing the hours away.

The war might have been won but the future of the town's dockyard had already been decided. And it was not good news for anyone. By the early months of 1919, it was not a case of whether or not the yards would close – it was simply a matter of when.

The writing had been on the wall since October 1904, when Jacky Fisher became First Sea Lord. It mattered not that his favourite ship, the *Renown*, was Pembroke-Dock built. It mattered not that, in 1878, he had been appointed Captain of the *Valorous*, launched from the dockyard in April 1851 as one of the last paddle warships in the navy. It mattered not that for fifty years Pembroke Dockyard had built Royal Yachts for the Queen. A supreme pragmatist, all that mattered to Jacky Fisher was the efficiency of the Royal Navy.

Fisher was a man of boundless energy, always totally convinced that there was only one way to go and only one opinion to count – his. He was the man behind the development of the *Dreadnought*, the navy's first turbine-driven battleship, armed with ten 12-inch guns instead of the usual four. She was a revolutionary vessel and effectively made every other capital ship in the world virtually obsolete overnight.

Jacky Fisher wanted all of the navy battleships armed with the largest and heaviest calibre weapons possible. Giant Dreadnoughts were the future and Pembroke Dockyard was simply not big enough to cope with the demand for ships of such size and complexity. The development of the battlecruiser concept in the years after 1907 – huge ships of enormous length – provided even more problems for Pembroke Dock.

With the trumpets already beginning to sound over the Imperial retreat and with naval treaties that limited the size and number of ships each nation was to possess, the number of light cruisers required by the RN was always going to be limited.

Admiral Jacky Fisher, First Sea Lord
and nemesis of Pembroke Dockyard
with his insistence on big gun
battleships. The Pembroke Dock
yards could not cope with such
vessels and from the early years of
the twentieth century closure was
always on the cards.

Fisher's dislike of gunboats ('too weak to fight, too slow to run away') has been well
recorded and as Pembroke Dockyard produced exactly this type of vessel, it was clear
to those who cared to look that the yards could not hope to survive for long.

With more and more commercial yards now able to produce warships quickly and
cheaply, the Royal Naval Dockyards were becoming more involved with fitting out
than ship building. Pembroke Dock had never been a great fitting out yard and to
convert it to such a purpose, building dry docks, fitting basins and deep water jetties,
would have been hugely expensive.

Although in early 1918 the yards were employing over 4,000 men – as well as 500
women – by the middle of 1919 the workforce at Pembroke Dock had been reduced
almost by half, workers being laid off on a regular basis. There really was not enough
work to keep them employed.

After the launch of the submarine H52 in 1918, over the next four years the yards
produced only two coal lighters and assisted in the building of the cruiser *Capetown*.

In a strange reversal of roles, the *Capetown* was launched from the yards of
Cammell Laird at Birkenhead in the summer of 1919 and then brought to Pembroke
Dock for completion. It was a bizarre effort to keep the workforce busy but the
dockyard maties knuckled down to their task and had duly finished the *Capetown* by
February 1922.

HMS *Capetown*, built at Cammell Laird's and at Pembroke Dockyard, is shown here passing an iceberg in northern waters.

The cruiser *Caroline*, built at Cammell Laird's – her sisters *Carysfort* and *Cordelia* were Pembroke Dock ships – came to the dockyard in the summer of 1919 where she was commissioned for service on the East Indies Station. It was not building work or even fitting out but her presence at the dockyard at least kept the ship's chandlers in business.

Moored, first, against Carr Jetty, then to various buoys out in the Haven, on Monday 30 June the ship's log recorded the laconic message:

To supper. Spliced mainbrace by order of Captain Law RN in honour of the signing of the Peace Treaty.[35]

This was the formal ending of the First World War, the ceasefire of the previous November having been simply an Armistice. Having loaded with ammunition and supplies, the *Caroline* soon slipped her moorings and headed out to sea.

The last ship to be built at Pembroke Dockyard was the RFA tanker *Oleander*. She came off the launching ways on 26 April 1922 but even then her boilers and much of her essential machinery had been made at other Royal Dockyards like Chatham and Devonport in an attempt to spread the workload and keep the yards going.

The *Oleander* was one of six ships in her class and, in the days of hardship and economic depression that followed the war, spent a lot of her life out on charter. In 1927 she was involved in a collision with the Royal Mail steamer *Nebraska* during a heavy fog in the English Channel. The accident left *Oleander* seriously damaged and leaking oil into the water.

In a strange, not to say bizarre incident, in October 1933 while undergoing a refit at Devonport, nuts and bolts were found in the machinery of the *Oleander*, causing her

H.M.S. " *Caroline* ", *Friday* 27ᵗʰ day of *June*, 19*19*.

From ___ , To ___ or At *Pembroke Dock*.

Time	Patent Log	Distance Run		True Course	Revolutions per minute	Wind			State of the Sea	Height of Barometer and attached Thermometer	Temperature			Position 0800 / 2000	Latitude	Longitude
		Miles	Tenths			Direction	Force	Weather			Air	Wet Bulb	Sea			

Time	Remarks
0100	
0200	
0300	
0400	Variable ... 30.20/60 53 51
0500	Ship commissioned by Captain W.J.B.
0600	Law, Royal Navy, for service on
	the East Indies Station;
0700	The Balance of crew having joined
	Ship from R.N. Barracks, Portsmouth
	on the previous evening at 9.15 p.m.
0800	Variable ... 30.20/61 55 54
0900	9.0 Hands employed cleaning
	ship, drawing stores from
1000	Dockyard &c as Reqᵗ.
1100	
Noon	NE 1 bc 30.20/62 62 58

Alongside Bar Jetty.
Pembroke Dock.

Distance run through the Water	Course and Distance made good	Latitude		Longitude		Number on Sick List	Provisions received		Fresh Water	
		D.R.		D.R.				lbs.		Tons
		Obs.		Obs.					Received	23
Time kept at Noon	True Bearing and Distance		Currents in the 24 hours ending at Noon				Fresh Meat		Distilled	
(Z-1) B.S.T.							Vegetables		Expended	7
							Bread		Remaining	34

Time	Remarks
	12.5 Ammunition lighter secured alongside
1300	1.30 Hands employed embarking
1400	ammunition as Reqᵗ.
1500	
1600	NE 1 bc 30.20/62 70 62
1700	5.40 Watch employed embarking provisions
1800	6.10 Slipped from Jetty & proceeded as Reqᵗ
1900	in charge of Pilot.
	6.45 Secured to "A" mooring buoy.
2000	NE 1 bc 30.20/61 62 59 leave to one watch till 7 am.
2100	9.0 Rounds
2200	
2300	
Midt	NE 1 oc 30.20/.. 58 62

0 5 as Reqᵗ

at "A" Buoy
Pembroke Dock.

Opposite page: A page from the ship's log of HMS *Caroline*, a cruiser commissioned, equipped and stored at Pembroke Dock in 1919 – but not built there – for service in the Far East.

Above: The last ship built in the Royal Naval Dockyard at Pembroke Dock, the RFA tanker *Oleander*. She was damaged and abandoned during the Norwegian Campaign of 1940.

main engines to fail. Deliberate sabotage was suspected but no culprit was ever found and the origin of the nuts remains unclear.

Following the launch of the *Oleander* Pembroke Dockyard lapsed into an uneasy and unhappy state of waiting. A serious fire in the mould loft of the dockyard on 24 July 1922 caused major damage, destroying an invaluable collection of ships figureheads and models. Archive records were also lost in the blaze.

The announcement that the Dockyard was to close came on Wednesday 2 September 1925. Many had feared it but nobody in the town really wanted to believe such a thing could happen. The town had been created to build ships, now its reason for existence was about to be snatched away.

Pembroke Dockyard, like Rosyth in Scotland, was to be reduced to what the Admiralty called 'a care and maintenance' standard. The yards were mothballed, plant and machinery being regularly overhauled in case there should ever be a need to use them again, but shipbuilding at Pembroke Dock had, for the moment, come to an end.

Words can say only so much. For the people of Pembroke Dock, many of whom relied on the dockyard for trade and business, the closure brought economic hardship on an unparalleled scale.

The Admiralty tried to soften the blow but it was scant consolation for the community. Established men would be offered redeployment to other dockyards but for casual or hired workers there was only the dole queue.

The fire at Pembroke Docks on June 24th 1922. photographed by J.H.Roberts. DrugStores, Neyland, from a distance of over one mile.

The Pier, Pembroke Dock.   Morgan, Pembroke Dock.

Above: In 1922 a serious fire broke out in the mould loft of the dockyard, serving to hasten the decline and eventual closure of the yards. This view of the fire was taken by J. H. Roberts of the Drug Store in Neyland – he had the shot on sale as a postcard by the end of the day.

Left: When the yards closed in 1926 the town was left without aim or design. It had been created to build ships for the navy, now that purpose had gone and the workmen could only stand and wonder what had gone wrong.

The building sheds are in the process of being demolished in this 1930s view of the town and dockyard.

Pembroke Dockyard was officially closed on 31 May 1926. The last Captain Superintendent was Leonard Donaldson, his appointment being terminated the day the yards were officially closed.

The dockyard had lasted only 112 years and in that time had produced many fine warships. The workmen had much to pride themselves about but, as soon became clear, the world had not quite finished with Pembroke Dock.

17

The Second World War

The outbreak of the Second World War brought Pembroke Dock a new lease of life, a second – if brief – chance of glory. A flying boat base had been created in the eastern part of the old dockyard in 1931 and by 1939 the Sunderlands of PD, as the base became known throughout the RAF, were ready to 'do their bit' for the war effort.

Throughout the war years the Sunderlands and Catalinas of PD operated long range missions out across the Atlantic and the Bay of Biscay. As much as any of the convoy escorts, these aircraft helped defeat the German U-Boat threat and when the air station finally closed in 1957 it was news that was received with much regret in the town. But in the early 1940s closure of the air base was far from people's minds.

In 1941 the old dockyard was re-opened, not as a ship building centre but as a very effective repair and refit yard. Together with the flying boat base, this made the town an ideal target for the Luftwaffe. Right to the end of the war the Germans thought this was still a major ship building dockyard and, as a consequence, the town was heavily bombed on many occasions.

The most dangerous moment came on Monday 19 August 1940, when three Junkers 88s flew in over the coast and deposited bombs onto the oil tank farm at Pennar above the town. Only one tank was hit but the fire quickly spread from one oil container to another and, in the end, eleven of the eighteen tanks were destroyed. Firemen from all over Wales and England arrived to help fight the blaze, five men from Cardiff being incinerated when the wall of one tank split open, covering the fire fighters in burning oil.

A huge cloud of smoke and oil had leapt into the air the moment the bombs dropped and hung above the town for two weeks as firemen fought to contain the flames. At the time it was the largest fire Britain had seen since the Great Fire of London in 1666. Of course, there were worse fires in places like Coventry, Liverpool and London in the years ahead but, at that moment in time, the oil tank blaze was a terrifying experience for Pembroke Dock firemen and civilians alike.

As if that was not enough, the Luftwaffe came back many times during the next few years and on the night of 12 May 1941, in a raid that lasted many hours, the town was virtually reduced to rubble. Incendiary bombs and high explosive fell onto

When the Royal Air Force established its flying boat base in the eastern half of the old dockyard in 1931 the original intention was to stay for only a few months. As it turned out they stayed for twenty-nine years.

The mighty Sunderland flying boat, a familiar sight for many years on the Haven off Pembroke Dock.

The cloud of smoke and debris that hung over Pembroke Dock's bombed and burning oil tanks in the summer of 1940 – like a sword of Damocles above the town. The tank fire burned for eighteen days.

Bomb damage in Gwyther Street, the morning after a raid.

the houses but, amazingly, the dockyard and flying boat base remained undamaged.[36] It was a frightening time for the people of Pembroke Dock but there was work to be done and the town and the dockyard carried on regardless.

Six Pembroke Dock ships were still afloat when war broke out on 3 September 1939. Of these, the old cruiser *Thames* was in Simonstown in South Africa, serving as an accommodation ship, her last useful service before heading for the breakers yards in 1947. The *Inconstant* was acting as a Training Ship at Plymouth, training sailors in the art of torpedo warfare, while the Royal Yacht *Victoria and Albert* had also been requisitioned as an accommodation ship for sailors.

The oiler *Oleander* had been the last ship launched from the Dockyard in April 1922. On 12 May 1940, during the Norway Campaign, she joined Convoy N53 heading into Harstad Bay. No fighter cover was available and that made the convoy an easy target for German dive bombers.

On 26 May the *Oleander*, in the company of aircraft carrier *Glorious*, was seriously damaged by air attack. No bombs actually struck the ship but several near misses forced her ashore, where she was abandoned. Three crewmen had been injured but the damage to the *Oleander* quickly proved to be fatal and on 8 June she was officially classified as a total loss. The wreck of this, the last of the Pembroke Dock ships, was visible for years afterwards, lying marooned and lonely on the rocky shore of the fjord.

The *Curacoa*, named after a West Indian island which was more usually spelled Curaçao, had been launched on 5 May 1917. Completed in February the following year, she was a fast ship capable of making 25 knots. Arguably, she represented the epitome, the zenith of cruiser building at Pembroke Dock, a beautiful and effective ship that was the height of grace and power.

Designed for scouting duties, she spent the final days of the Great War with the Grand Fleet in Scapa Flow before going on to serve in the Baltic in 1919, where she had the misfortune to strike a mine. Quickly repaired, she was soon on duty in the Mediterranean and the Far East.

In 1935, along with three other RN ships, the *Curacoa* appeared in the film *Brown on Resolution*, an adaptation of the C. S. Forester novel of the same name, when she featured as a German battlecruiser.

The growth of air power in the inter-war years had been phenomenal and in the final years before the Second World War broke out, the *Curacoa* was re-fitted with eight 4-inch and multiple pom-pom guns in front of her bridge, ready for a new role as an anti-aircraft ship. She was damaged during the Norway Campaign but was quickly repaired and sent on escort duties in the Atlantic.

On 2 October 1942, while engaged in these escort duties, the *Curacoa* was rammed and sunk by the liner *Queen Mary*. The affair was a catalogue of disasters right from the beginning, as communications between the two ships was poor and the liner's compass was off by two degrees. Significantly, officers on the *Queen Mary*'s bridge failed to inform the *Curacoa* about her zig-zag patterns.

There had already been several close calls but finally, at 2.12 p.m. the *Queen Mary* sliced through the cruiser, cutting her in half. The stern section of the mortally

H. M. S. "CURACOA"

Warship, film star and, eventually, victim of the liner *Queen Mary*– the cruiser *Curacoa*, launched from the dockyard in May 1917.

wounded *Curacoa* sank almost immediately but the bow half partly righted itself and for a moment or two Captain Boutwood thought that his ship might be saved. It was not to be and the bow section soon slipped under the waves.

The *Queen Mary*, travelling fast and independently – as far as possible – across the Atlantic, had orders not to stop and so Captain Illingworth and the liner simply proceeded on their way. It was left to nearby destroyers to pick up survivors.

The rescue operation took over four hours and out of the crew of 439 only 101 survived. Although the *Queen Mary* suffered damage to a bulkhead that kept her in dry dock for a short while, many of the men on board had no idea what had happened. Many of them simply thought that they had hit a large wave.

After the war a Court of Inquiry was held into the accident. Initially, the disaster was blamed on Captain Boutwood and the *Curacoa* but after an appeal by the Admiralty it was decided that the fault lay two-thirds with the *Curacoa*, one-third with the *Queen Mary*.

The final Pembroke Dock ship still afloat during these wartime years was the *Capetown*, which had been partly built in the yards and launched by Cammel Laird of Birkenhead in 1922.

A rugged and sturdy little ship, built for the rough conditions of the North Sea, she was armed with five 6-inch and two 3-inch guns. Apart from the *Capetown* and her sister ship *Colombo*, all other ships in her class were converted to anti-aircraft vessels in the early days of the war. The *Capetown* did, however, receive an additional six 20-mm weapons to help her deal with aerial attack and she was also fitted with radar.

The *Capetown*, completed at Pembroke Dock but laid down and launched at Cammell Laird's yard in Birkenhead.

On 6 April 1941, off Eritrea, she was torpedoed by the Italian motor torpedo boat MAS 213. Brought into Sudan under tow by the Australian sloop *Parramatta*, she was under repair at Bombay for twelve months. She was ready for the D-Day landings on 6 June 1944, bombarding German positions prior to the troops landing.

Like so many other ships, after the war *Capetown* was considered surplus to requirements and was sold for breaking on 5 April 1946.

18

Private Shipyards

There had always been a great deal of ship building along the Milford Haven waterway. Such activity existed long before the arrival of Pembroke Dockyard, it continued during the time the yards were working and, in a low key sort of way, it continued after they closed in 1926.

Some of the building was government sponsored. In particular, two ships, the *Milford* and the *Prince of Wales*, had been built for the navy by Richard Chitty at Neyland – or New Milford as it was later intended to be called – in 1759 and 1765 respectively. The arrival of Milford and Pembroke Dock as ship building centres effectively ended such semi-official initiatives but private enterprises continued to flourish.

Perhaps the most successful of these private yards was at Jacobs Pill, on the banks of Pembroke River, a bare 1½ miles from Pembroke Dockyard. Officially known as the Milford Haven Shipbuilding & Engineering Company, the building yard was founded in the 1870s by Sir Edward Reed, one time Chief Constructor for the navy – designer of many Pembroke Dock ships – and Member of Parliament for Pembroke Boroughs.

As chairman of the company, Reed used his influence to gain an order from the Imperial Japanese Government for an armoured warship. This was the corvette *Hei-Yei*. She was the first in a long procession of ships that would take the Japanese navy from being an essentially sail-powered force to a position where its warships dominated the eastern oceans. Many years later, but for a stroke of ill fortune, the Japanese Fleet could well have destroyed virtually the whole the American Navy at Pearl Harbour.

A three masted, barque rigged ship, the *Hei-Yei* was also steam powered and screw driven. Armed with six 5.9-inch and three 6.7-inch guns, she was also equipped with torpedo tubes and numerous Nordenfeldt machine guns. The day of her launch, 11 June 1877, was one of spectacular pomp and ceremony.

His Excellency Jushie Wooyeno Kagenori, Envoy Extraordinary and Minister Plenipotentiary to the Mikado, arrived at Pembroke Dock to witness the launch. Greeted at the railway station by cheering crowds – most of whom had never laid eyes on anyone from Japan before – he was driven to Jacobs Pill in an open carriage,

All that now remains of Jacobs Pill Dockyard on Pembroke River, the foundations of the lock gates and a metal pin – a sad end for the yards that built a warship for the Japanese Navy.

hundreds of people lining the streets and then rushing to the banks of Pembroke River to watch the launch.

To the sound of three bands and several choirs, the daughter of James Reed duly christened the ship and the *Hei-Yei* slipped into the river. The official party then headed back into Pembroke Dock – stopping on the way to unveil a memorial plaque on Bethany Chapel – for a banquet at the Victoria Hotel. The day was finished with a massive firework display on the slopes of the Barrack Hill.

After fitting out, a British crew took the *Hei-Yei* to Yokashuka, where she arrived on 22 May 1878. Several Japanese sailors were on board, however, including the future Admiral Togo Heihachiro, soon to be the victor at the Battle of Tsushima. He had been studying on board the training ship *Worcester* on the Thames, even though he was, technically, too old for admission and had to lie about his age, and was now ready to return to Japan.

The *Hei-Yei* undertook several long distance cruises for the Imperial Navy and saw combat in the First Sino-Japanese War. She was damaged at the Battle of Yahu River and took part in the invasion of Taiwan. During the Russo-Japanese War she was guard ship at Port Arthur.

The real significance of the ship, however, lay not in her career but in what she represented – Japan's first venture into the world of modern sea warfare. And to think that she was built in a tiny dockyard on the Pembroke River!

Jacobs Pill went on to build seven more small ships, notably colliers such as the *Rhiwbina*, built in 1882 for John Cory & Sons of Cardiff, the *Rowan* and the *Milford*.

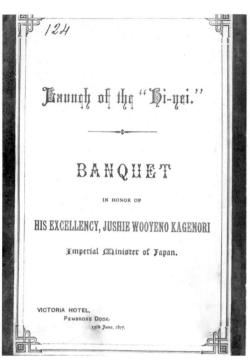

Launch of the "Hi-yei."

BANQUET

IN HONOR OF

HIS EXCELLENCY, JUSHIE WOOYENO KAGENORI

Imperial Minister of Japan.

VICTORIA HOTEL,
PEMBROKE DOCK.
13th June, 1877.

Left: The cover for the banquet menu after the launch of the *Hei-Yei*.

Below: The menu for the celebration dinner after the launch of the *Hei-Yei* at Jacobs Pill. The dinner was held at the Victoria Hotel in the town – a rich spread indeed.

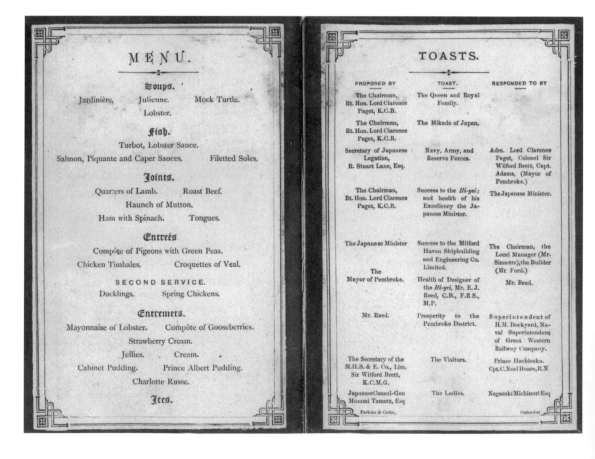

MENU.

Soups.

Jardinière.   Julienne.   Mock Turtle.

Lobster.

Fish.

Turbot, Lobster Sauce.

Salmon, Piquante and Caper Sauces.   Filetted Soles.

Joints.

Quarters of Lamb.   Roast Beef.

Haunch of Mutton.

Ham with Spinach.   Tongues.

Entrees

Compôte of Pigeons with Green Peas.

Chicken Timbales.   Croquettes of Veal.

SECOND SERVICE.

Ducklings.   Spring Chickens.

Entremets.

Mayonnaise of Lobster.   Compôte of Gooseberries.

Strawberry Cream.

Jellies.   Cream.

Cabinet Pudding.   Prince Albert Pudding.

Charlotte Russe.

Ices.

TOASTS.

PROPOSED BY	TOAST.	RESPONDED TO BY
The Chairman, Rt. Hon. Lord Clarence Paget, K.C.B.	The Queen and Royal Family.	
The Chairman, Rt. Hon. Lord Clarence Paget, K.C.B.	The Mikado of Japan.	
Secretary of Japanese Legation, R. Stuart Lane, Esq.	Navy, Army, and Reserve Forces.	Adm. Lord Clarence Paget, Colonel Sir Wilford Brett, Capt. Adams, (Mayor of Pembroke.)
The Chairman, Rt. Hon. Lord Clarence Paget, K.C.B.	Success to the *Hi-yei*; and health of his Excellency the Japanese Minister.	The Japanese Minister.
The Japanese Minister	Success to the Milford Haven Shipbuilding and Engineering Co. Limited.	The Chairman, the Local Manager (Mr. Sinnette),the Builder (Mr. Ford.)
The Mayor of Pembroke.	Health of Designer of the *Hi-yei*, Mr. E.J. Reed, C.B., F.R.S., M.P.	Mr. Reed.
Mr. Reed.	Prosperity to the Pembroke District.	Superintendent of H.M. Dockyard, Naval Superintendent of Great Western Railway Company.
The Secretary of the M.H.S. & E. Co., Lim. Sir Wilford Brett, K.C.M.G.	The Visitors.	Prince Hachisuka, Cpt. C. Noel Houre, R.N
Japanese Consul-Gen Minami Tamotz, Esq	The Ladies.	Nagasaki Michinori Esq

Parkins & Gotto.   Oxford-st

A faded and almost ghostly old photograph showing the assembled dignitaries and officials of Jacobs Pill at the launch of the *Hei-Yei*.

A newspaper cutting, faded and old, showing the *Hei-Yei* in Pembroke River.

In 1884 the yards launched a 970-ton sloop, the *Acorn*, for the Royal Navy but perhaps its most notable achievement was the building of the caisson gate for nearby Milford Docks. This iron gate was in regular and almost constant use until it was finally taken away in 1998.

The last vessel built at Jacobs Pill was the *Mary Jane Lewis*, launched in 1889. She ended her days abandoned on the foreshore at East Angle Bay, just a dozen miles to the west of her place of birth. Jacobs Pill closed soon after work on the *Mary Jane Lewis* was completed, its order books empty and the slipways left to ruin.

The old mould loft for the dockyard was later converted into an isolation hospital for Pembroke Dock but this closed soon after the Second World War. Now all that remains of a fascinating, if short-lived, business venture are a few old walls and some very faded photographs of the day a senior Japanese minister came to help launch a ship.

At one time or another there were a number of other private shipbuilding yards in Pembroke Dock. One of these was the firm of Robertson's in Front Street. Between 1831 and 1839 they built six small vessels, most notably the *Resolution* which was lost in the Atlantic while carrying timber from America.

The firm of J. D. Warlow built no fewer than twenty-two vessels between 1868 and 1909 and there were several more private companies that came and went fairly quickly during the Victorian and Edwardian periods.

Peter Hancock & Sons began ship building in Front Street in 1921. Between then and 1979, when the yards closed, they built eighteen vessels. In particular, in 1956 and 1962 they launched the ferry boats *Cleddau Queen* and *Cleddau King* for Pembrokeshire County Council.

Ferries had plied their trade across the Haven, from Hobbs Point to Neyland, for many years. Vessels like the *Amy* and the *Pioneer* had given way to the *Alumchine* and the *Lady Magdalene*, all of them becoming much loved sights and a part of Pembroke Dock life. The *Cleddau Queen* and *Cleddau King* were the last of the line. The *Queen* was an oil-fired paddler launched in January 1956, the *King*, with her ramp access being an unusual but effective diesel-powered ship that began operations six years later. The *King* remained in service until the Cleddau Bridge was built across the river, her last fare-paying trip being made on 8 March 1975.

Perhaps one of the most significant attempts to breathe life back into Pembroke Dock as a ship building town was made by the firm of R. S. Hayes. In the years after the Second World War Hayes rented part of the old dockyard and began a ship repair company. In 1955 they converted a former German cargo vessel, the *Empire Frome*, into the cable ship *Ocean Layer*.

The firm had already built and launched the *Ramos*, a twin-screw tug, and in 1956 they completed the trawler *Norrard Star*. Last used in 1991, she was sold a year later. Hayes then diversified into rope running for the tankers at the various Milford Haven oil terminals and ship building at Pembroke Dock finally came to an end.

The *Cleddau King*
approaching Hobbs Point.
Notice the increased number
of cars carried, a sure sign
that some quicker and more
effective way across the Haven
was needed. The answer was
to build a bridge.

Building the ferry *Cleddau
Queen*, the last steam paddle
ship to be built in Britain, in
the dry dock of Hancocks
yard in Pembroke Dock,
c. 1965.

The *Cleddau Queen* at Hobbs
Point.

The *Cleddau Queen* in use. (*J&C McCutcheon Collection*)

The *Ocean Layer*, a cable layer, was converted from a German cargo vessel by the firm of R. S. Hayes in 1955.

The motor vessel *Kirtondike* slips into the water of the Haven. Built by R. S. Hayes she provided almost the last vestiges of ship building in Pembroke Dock.

19

Conclusion

When the people of Pembroke Dock celebrated the centenary of their town on 15 July 1914 they had little idea that within the month Britain would be at war with Germany. They did not – could not – know that many of the ships of which they were so proud would soon be facing a violent and implacable foe or that so many men from the town would perish on the fields of northern France or in far-flung places like Gallipoli and Palestine.

So they unveiled their centenary monument, took part in races and confetti battles and sang and danced the night away in the town's Market Hall, blissfully unaware of what was about to be unleashed on the world.

They were even less aware that in the short space of twelve years their dockyard would be closed and thousands thrown onto the dole. The town had been created to build ships – it was unthinkable that the sole purpose of its existence should be smashed away.

And yet, that is exactly what happened. With the launch of the *Oleander* in 1922 ship building at Pembroke Dock more or less came to an end. Private yards continued, of course, but they could not begin to fill the gap created by the departure of the Royal Naval Dockyard.

There were some compensations, mostly in things like the RAF flying boat base and, for a while at least, the continued presence of the military. Soldiers had originally come to protect the dockyard, living and working in one of three large barracks on the hills above the town. They stayed until 1966.

And as late as 1979 there was a strange but fascinating interlude when the *Millennium Falcon*, a spaceship for the *Star Wars* series of films, was built in one of the old hangars in the eastern part of the dockyard. The strange ship could not fly or float but was, apparently, able to hover a few feet above the floor. Quite what the shipwrights and fitters of Pembroke Dockyard would have made of it is best left to conjecture.

Now all that remains are the memories, memories and the dreams of glory about what was once an important and impressive centre of industry and trade. It was the only Royal Naval Dockyard to exist in Wales and once drew the comment from Philip

Right: The people of Pembroke Dock celebrated the centenary of the town in July 1914, little realising that within the month Britain would be at war – within twelve years the dockyard would be shut. This postcard view shows the centenary monument in Albion Square in the town.

Below: Pembroke Dockyard as it should be remembered with gigantic building sheds lining the water's edge and plenty of activity in the Haven.

Perhaps the greatest ship ever launched from Pembroke Dockyard, the mighty *Duke of Wellington*.

Dockyard workers on board one of the ships. After 1926 this was a sight that nobody in Pembroke Dock would see again.

A mid-Victorian print showing the dockyard in its heyday, at the height of its glory and power – a far cry from the sad closure of 1926.

Hichborn, Chief Constructor of the US Navy, that although the scope of the yards was limited (due mainly to the fact that they had just one wet basin and no real fitting out berths), this was 'the finest ship building yard in the world.'

He was probably right. In an age when experiment and revolutionary changes in design dominated the ship building world, Pembroke Dockyard was renowned for the quality of its workers and of its workmanship. They didn't always get it right. Not every ship was an unmitigated success but every single one of them played a part in making the Royal Navy the envy of the world.

The *Hannibal* and *Duke of Wellington*, the *Erebus* and the *Drake*, the *Renown* and the *Carysfort*, they became household names. And so did many others, too. They created a panoply or rich tapestry, ships that were symbolic of the Victorian navy.

And that is why the ships – as well as the dockyard and the town – deserve to be remembered. They, after all, were what the dockyard was really all about.

Appendix: Ships Built in the Royal Naval Dockyard at Pembroke Dock

This list has been compiled from a number of sources and is as full as the author can possibly make it. However, it does not purport to be a complete listing, with 100 per cent accuracy. Other ships will undoubtedly be added in the years to come:

Name Type Launch Date Comments

Ariadne Frigate/Sixth Rate 10 Feb 1816 First PD ship

Valorous Frigate/Sixth Rate 10 Feb 1816

Thetis Frigate/Fifth Rate 1 Feb 1817 Wrecked off Brazil

Arethusa Frigate/Fifth Rate 29 July 1817

Racer Cutter 4 April 1818 Built undercover

Sprightly Cutter 3 June 1818

Belleisle Line of Battle Ship 26 April 1819 74-gun ship

Fisguard Frigate/Fifth Rate 8 July 1819

Frolic Sloop 10 June 1820

Falcon Sloop 10 June 1820

Melampus Frigate/Fifth Rate 10 Aug 1820

Nereus Frigate?Fifth Rate 30 July 1821

Reynard Sloop 26 Oct 1821

Meteor Bomb Ship 25 June 1823

Hamadryad Frigate/Fifth Rate 25 July 1823 Hospital Ship at Cardiff

Zephyr Brig 1 Nov 1823

Wellington Lighter 28 June 1824

Vengeance Line of Battle Ship 27 July 1824 84-gun Second Rate

Thisbe Frigate 9 Sept 1824 Gospel Ship at Cardiff

Talbot Frigate/Sixth Rate 9 Oct 1824

Sheldrake Sloop 19 May 1825

Druid Frigate 1 July 1825

Success Frigate 30 Aug 1825

Skylark Sloop 16 May 1826

Erebus Bomb Ship 7 June 1826 Converted to exploration ship

Nemesis Frigate 19 Aug 1826

Satellite Sloop 2 Oct 1826

Mooring Lighter Lighter 27 Dec 1826

Clarence Line of Battle Ship 25 July 1827 84-gun Second Rate

Spey Sloop 6 Oct 1827

Variable Sloop 6 Oct 1827

Leda Frigate 15 April 1828

Sparrow Cutter 28 June 1828

Snipe Cutter 28 June 1828

Speedy Cutter 28 June 1828

Comet Sloop 11 Aug 1828

Hotspur Frigate 9 Oct 1828

Lightning Sloop 2 June 1829 Renamed *Larne* 1829

Partridge Sloop 12 Oct 1829

Thais Sloop 12 Oct 1829

Raven Cutter 21 Oct 1829 Survey Vessel

Starling Sloop 31 Oct 1829

Wizard Sloop 24 May 1830

Sea Horse Frigate 21 July 1830

Stag Frigate 2 Oct 1830

Timber Barge Barge 29 Jan 1831

Viper Sloop 12 May 1831

Imogene Frigate 24 June 1831

Fly Sloop 25 Aug 1831

Harrier Sloop 8 Nov 1831

Cockatrice Sloop 14 May 1832

Andromache Frigate 27 Aug 1832

Royal William Line of Battle Ship 2 April 1833 120-gun First Rate

Rodney Line of Battle Ship 18 June 1833 92-gun Second Rate

Forth Frigate 1 Aug 1833

Foundation Water Lighter 26 Nov 1833

Sinbad Lighter 27 Feb 1834

Tartarus Steam Paddler 23 June 1834 First PD
  steamship

Cleopatra Frigate 28 April 1835

Vanguard Line of Battle Ship 25 Aug 1835 78-
  gun Third Rate

Harlequin Sloop 18 March 1836

Dido Sloop/Corvette 13 June 1836

Carysfort Frigate 12 Aug 1836

Cremill Victualling Hoy 29 Aug 1836

Gorgon Steam Frigate 31 Aug 1837 Wooden
  steam-paddler

Lily Sloop/Brig 28 Sept 1837

Penguin Mail Brig 10 April 1838

Grecian Sloop 28 April 1838

Petrel Mail Brig 23 May 1838

Daphne Sloop 6 Aug 1838

Merlin Mail Brig 18 Sept 1838

Medusa Mail Packet 31 Oct 1838

Cyclops Steam Frigate 10 July 1839 Wooden
  steam-paddler

Persian Frigate 7 Oct 1839

Medina Mail Packet 18 March 1840

Iris Frigate 14 July 1840

Vixen Steam Sloop 4 Feb 1841

Geyser Paddle Sloop 6 April 1841

Cambrian Frigate 5 July 1841

Collingwood Battleship 17 Aug 1841 80-gun
  Third Rate

Spiteful Steam Sloop 24 March 1842

Superb Battleship 16 Sept 1842 80-gun Third
  Rate

Victoria & Albert Royal Yacht 26 April 1843
  First Royal Yacht at PD

Helena Sloop 11 July 1843

Vulture Steam Frigate 21 Sept 1843

Flying Fish Brig 3 April 1844

Centurion Battleship 2 May 1844 80-gun
  Third Rate

Juno Frigate 1 July 1844 Renamed *Atalanta*

Tank Vessel Water Vessel 21 Aug 1844

Kingfisher Brig 18 April 1845

Harrier Wooden Screw Sloop 13 May 1845

Inflexible Frigate 22 May 1845

Dragon Paddle Frigate 17 July 1845

Constance Frigate 12 March 1846

Conflict Screw Sloop 5 Aug 1846

Encounter Screw Sloop 24 Sept 1846

Mariner Brig 19 Oct 1846

Sybille Frigate 15 April 1847

Britomart Sloop 12 June 1847

Lion Battleship 29 July 1847 80-gun Second
  Rate

Camilla Sloop 8 Sept 1847

Atalanta Brig 19 Oct 1847 Name given to *Juno*

Colossus Battleship 1 July 1848

Magicienne Paddle Frigate 2 March 1849

Buzzard Paddle Sloop 24 March 1849

Desperate Screw Sloop 23 May 1849

Arethusa Frigate 20 June 1849

Octavia Frigate 18 Aug 1849

Liberty Training Brig 1 June 1850

Marten Brig/Training Brig 19 Sept 1850
  Renamed *Kingfisher*

Barracouta Paddle Sloop 31 March 1851

Valorous Paddle Frigate 30 April 1851 Last
  steam-paddler in RN

Mosquito Brig 20 July 1851

Duke of Wellington Battleship 14 Sept 1852
  Largest woodenwall

James Watt Battleship 23 April 1853

Rover Brig 21 June 1853

Caesar Battleship 7 Aug 1853

Squirrel Sloop 8 Aug 1853

Curacoa Screw Frigate 13 April 1854

Swallow Screw Sloop 12 June 1854

Ariel Screw Sloop 11 July 1854

Falcon Screw Sloop 10 Aug 1854

Victoria & Albert Royal Yacht 16 Jan 1855
  PD's second Royal Yacht

Sutlej Frigate 17 April 1855

Brunswick Battleship 1 June 1855

Repulse Battleship 27 Sept 1855

Flying Fish Despatch Vessel 20 Dec 1855

Pioneer Gunboat 19 Jan 1856

Pet Gunboat 9 Feb 1856

Nettle Gunboat 9 Feb 1856

Rambler Gunboat 21 Feb 1856

Decoy Gunboat 21 Feb 1856

Janus Gunboat 8 March 1856

Drake Gunboat 8 March 1856 Same ship as
  Janus

Alert Sloop 20 May 1856 Exploration ship

Cordelia Screw Sloop 3 July 1856

Diadem Frigate 14 Oct 1856

Doris Frigate 25ᵗ March 1857

Melpomene Screw Frigate 8 August 1857

Gannet Sloop 29 Dec 1857

Orlando Screw Frigate 12 June 1858

Windsor Castle Battleship 26 August 1858

Revenge Battleship 16 April 1859

Greyhound Screw Sloop 15 June 1859

Immortalite Screw Frigate 25 Oct 1859

Espoir Gunboat 7 Jan 1860

Howe Battleship 7 March 1860 Last three-
  decker built

Pelican Screw Sloop 19 July 1860

Nimble Gunboat 15 Sept 1860

Pandora Gunboat 7 Feb 1861

Defiance Battleship 27 March 1861 Became
  torpedo school

Aurora Frigate 22 June 1861

Perseus Screw Sloop 21 Aug 1861

Shearwater Sloop 17 Oct 1861

Psyche Despatch Vessel 29 March 1862

Prince Consort Ironclad 29 June 1862 PD's first ironclad

Enchantress Admiralty Yacht 2 Aug 1862

Research Iron Screw Sloop 15 Aug 1863

N.B: Several orders were cancelled in 1863, due to the launch of the ironclad *Warrior*. The *Blake*, a 91-gun wooden battleship, had been laid down at Pembroke Dock and partially built but work was stopped this year when the Admiralty decided to build no more wooden warships.

Alberta Queen's Passage Boat 3 Oct 1863

Zealous Ironclad Frigate 7 March 1864

Lord Clyde Battleship 13 Oct 1864

Amazon Screw Sloop 23 May 1865

Vestal Screw Sloop 16 Nov 1865

Nassau Sloop 20 Feb 1866

Daphne Sloop 23 Oct 1866

Penelope Armour Clad Corvette 18 June 1867

Newport Gunboat 20 July 1867 Exploration ship

Gnat Composite Gunboat 26 Nov 1867

Inconstant Frigate 12 Nov 1868 Last PD ship afloat

Bittern Gunboat 20 Sept 1869

Iron Duke Battleship 1 March 1870

Osborne Royal Yacht 9 Dec 1870

Coquette Composite Gunboat 5 April 1871

Foam Composite Gunboat 29 Aug 1871

Decoy Composite Gunboat 12 Oct 1871

Merlin Composite Gunboat 24 Nov 1871

Mosquito Composite Gunboat 9 Dec 1871

Goshawk Composite Gunboat 23 Jan 1872

Swinger Composite Gunboat 7 Feb 1872

Thunderer Battleship 25 March 1872 Later guardship at PD

Sea Flower Training Brig 25 Feb 1873

Fantome Composite Gunboat 26 March 1873

Egeria Composite Gunboat 11 Nov 1873 Survey ship

Vesuvius Iron Torpedo Vessel 24 March 1874

Dreadnought Battleship 8 March 1875

Shannon Ironclad Battleship 11 Dec 1875

Emerald Composite Gunboat 18 Aug 1876

Iris Second Class Cruiser 12 April 1877 PD's first steel ship

Mercury Second Class Cruiser 17 April 1877 Sister ship to *Iris*

Pincher Iron Screw Gunboat 5 May 1879

Gadfly Iron Screw Gunboat 5 May 1879

Nautilus Training Brig 20 May 1879

Griper Iron Screw Gunboat 15 Sept 1879

Tickler Iron Screw Gunboat 15 Sept 1879

Pilot Training Brig 2 Nov 1879

Ajax Battleship 10 March 1880

Redwing Cutter (Coastguard?) 22 May 1880

Bullfrog Composite Gunboat 4 Feb 1881

Cockchafer Composite Gunboat 19 Feb 1881

Insolent Iron Gunboat 15 March 1881

Bouncer Steel Gunboat 15 March 1881

Edinburgh Battleship 18 March 1882

Collingwood Battleship 22 Nov 1882

Amphion Second Class Cruiser 13 Oct 1883

Howe Battleship 28 April 1885 Admiral Class

Thames Second Class Cruiser 3 Dec 1885 Later Sub Depot Ship

Anson Battleship 17 Feb 1886

Forth Second Class Cruiser 23 Oct 1886

Aurora Steel Cruiser 28 Oct 1887

Nile Battleship 27 March 1888

Peacock Composite Gunboat 22 June 1888

Pigeon Composite Gunboat 5 Sept 1888

Plover Composite Gunboat 18 Oct 1888

Magpie Composite Gunboat 15 March 1889

Redbreast Composite Gunboat 25 April 1889

Redpole Composite Gunboat 3 June 1889

Wigeon Composite Gunboat 9 Aug 1889

Blanche Third Class Cruiser 6 Sept 1889

Blonde Third Class Cruiser 22 Oct 1889 Last Composite Cruiser

Mayflower Training Brig 20 Jan 1890 PD's last wooden ship

Pearl Second Class Cruiser 28 July 1890

Empress of India Battleship 7 May 1891

Repulse Battleship 29 Feb 1892

Cambrian Second Class Cruiser 30 Jan 1893

Flora Second Class Cruiser 21 Nov 1893

Hazard Torpedo Gunboat 17 Feb 1894 Sunk 1918

Renown Battleship 8 May 1895

Hannibal Battleship 28 April 1896 PD's last battleship

Andromeda Cruiser 30 April 1897

Spartiate Cruiser 27 Oct 1898

Victoria & Albert Royal Yacht 9 May 1899 PD's last Royal Yacht

Drake Cruiser 5 March 1901 Longest ship at PD

Essex Cruiser 29 Aug 1910

Cornwall Cruiser 29 Oct 1902

Duke of Edinburgh Cruiser 14 June 1904

Warrior Cruiser 25 Nov 1905 Sunk at Jutland

Defence Cruiser 27 April 1907 Sunk at Jutland

Boadicea Scout Cruiser 14 May 1908

Bellona Scout Cruiser 20 March 1909

Blanche Scout Cruiser 25 Nov 1909

Blonde Scout Cruiser 22 July 1910

Active Scout Cruiser 14 March 1911

Amphion Scout Cruiser 4 Dec 1911 Sunk Aug 1914

Fearless Scout Cruiser 2 June 1912
Nottingham Light Cruiser 18 April 1913
Trefoil RFA Tanker 27 Oct 1913
Cordelia Light Cruiser 23 Feb 1914
Carysfort Light Cruiser 19 Nov 1914
J3 Submarine 4 Dec 1915 First Sub at PD
J4 Submarine 2 Feb 1916
Cambrian Light Cruiser 3 March 1916
Turmoil RFA Tanker 7 March 1917
Curacoa Light Cruiser 5 May 1917 Sunk by
    Queen Mary
L10 Submarine 24 Jan 1918 Sunk Oct 1918
H51 Submarine 15 Nov 1918
H52 Submarine 31 March 1919
Capetown Light Cruiser N/A – Launched by
    Cammell Laird
Oleander RFA Tanker 26 April 1922 Last ship
    built at PD

Notes/References

1.	Caryl Phillips *Foreigners*,	p. 30
2.	Phil Carradice *Nautical Training Ships*,	p. 32
3.	Phil Carradice *The History of Pembroke Dock*,	p. 21
4.	Ibid,	p. 24
5.	John Winton *Hurrah For the Life of a Sailor*,	p. 15
6.	C. S. Forester *Mr Midshipman Hornblower*,	p. 92
7.	Phil Carradice *Nautical Training Ships*,	p.152
8.	*Liverpool Daily Post*, 18 Jan 1884	
9.	*Liverpool Echo*, 17 Jan 1884	
10.	Phil Carradice *Nautical Training Ships*, p.	153
11.	Ibid,	p. 62-63
12.	Article in *Pembroke County Guardian*, 15 Sept 1869	
13.	Ibid	
14.	Ted Goddard *A Hero Bows Out*, article in *Pembrokeshire Life*, Sept 2012	
15.	Dr John Maybery *I Saw Three Ships*.	
16.	Ibid	
17.	Article in *The Times*, Sept 1846	
18.	Cissy, Countess of Denbigh, quoted in *The Faber Book of Reportage*,	p. 413
19.	GM Davis *The Loss of HMS Montagu*,	p. 26
20.	Commander J. S. Guard, unpublished article.	
21.	*Cruisers in Camera*,	p. 21
22.	Richard Brooks *The Long Arm of Empire*,	p. VIII
23.	Ibid,	p. VIII
24.	Julia Lovell *The Opium War*,	p. 91
25.	Quoted in *Hurrah For the Life of a Sailor*.	
26.	Robert Massie *Dreadnought*,	p. 433
27.	Ibid,	p. 448
28.	Christopher Lloyd *The British Seaman*,	p. 273
29.	HM Le Fleming *Warships of WW1*	
30.	Richard Hough *The Fleet That Had to Die*,	p. 49
31.	Article in *The Navy and Army Illustrated*, Sept 17 1898	
32.	Richard Hough,	p. 24
33.	H. M. Le Fleming,	p. 63
34.	Phil Carradice *Pembroke Dock in Old Postcards*,	p. 15
35.	Ships Log HMS *Caroline*	
36.	Phil Carradice *The History of Pembroke Dock*,	p. 182

Bibliography

PRIMARY SOURCES

Report on the State of Pembroke Dockyard, 1843
Ships Log HMS *Caroline*, June 1919
Unpublished article/paper by Commander J. S. Guard, undated

NEWSPAPERS/MAGAZINES

The Army and Navy Illustrated, 17 Sept 1898
Liverpool Daily Post, 18 Jan 1884
Liverpool Echo, 17 Jan 1884
Pembroke County Guardian, 15 Sept 1869
Pembrokeshire Life, Sept 2012
The Times – various for Sept 1846 and July 1859

BOOKS/SECONDARY SOURCES

Anon *The Guntower*, Pembs County Council, undated
Richard Brooks *The Long Arm of Empire*, Constable, 1999
John Carey (ed) *The Faber Book of Reportage,* Faber, 1987
Phil Carradice *The History of Pembroke Dock*, Accent Press, 2006
Nautical Training Ships, Amberley, 2009
Pembroke Dock in Old Postcards, European Library, 1992
G. M. Davis *The Loss of HMS Montagu*, privately printed, 1981
C. S. Forester *Mr Midshipman Hornblower*, Michael Joseph, 1951
Richard Hough *The Fleet That Had to Die*, New English Library, 1969
Richard Humble *Battleships and Battlecruisers*, Connoisseur, 1983
H. M. Le Fleming *Warships of WW1*, Ian Allan, undated
Christopher Lloyd *The British Seaman*, Collins, 1968
Julia Lovell *The Opium War*, Picador, 2011
Philip MacDougall *Royal Dockyards*, Shire, 1989
Robert Massie *Dreadnought*, Pimlico, 1993
Dr John Maybery *I Saw Three Ships*, Silver Link Publishing, undated
Keith Middlemass *Command the Far Seas*, Hutchinson, 1961
James Morris *Heaven's Command*, Penguin, 1979
Pax Britannica, Penguin, 1979
Caryl Phillips *Foreigners*, Vintage, 2008
A. B. Sainsbury/F. L. Phillips *The Royal Navy Day by Day*, Sutton, 2005
Wilfred Trotter *The Royal Navy in Old Photographs,* Dent, 1975
Spencer C. Tucker *Naval Warfare*, Sutton, 2000
Anthony J. Watts *Pictorial History of the Royal Navy,* Ian Allan, 1971
John Winton *Hurrah For the Life of a Sailor*, Michael Joseph, 1977

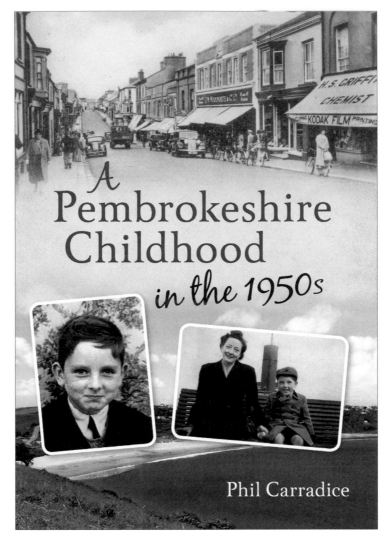

A Pembrokeshire Childhood in the 1950s
Phil Carradice

Phil Carradice's account of growing up in Pembrokeshire after the
Second World War ended.

978 1 4456 1311 6
128 pages